GAYS LESBIANS & FAMILY VALUES

GAYS LESBIANS & FAMILY VALUES

Elizabeth A. Say and Mark R. Kowalewski

The Pilgrim Press
Cleveland, Ohio

The Pilgrim Press, Cleveland, Ohio 44115

Printed in the United States of America on acid-free paper

03 02 01 00 99 98 5 4 3 2 1

Library of Congress Cataloging-in-Publication Data
Say, Elizabeth A.
Gays, lesbians, and family values / Elizabeth A. Say and Mark R. Kowalewski.
p. cm.
Includes bibliographical references (p.) and index.
ISBN 0-8298-1288-1 (pbk. : alk. paper)
1. Gays—United States—Family relationships. 2. Family—United States. 3. Interpersonal relations—United States. I. Kowalewski, Mark R., 1957– . II. Title.
HQ76.3.U5S39 1998
306.85—dc21 98-26773
CIP

Contents

Preface

In the past several years political and religious rhetoric has focused on what are termed family values. Both conservatives and liberals have engaged the family values debate, and both have sought to claim this ideological territory as their own. For the most part, however, such debates have not moved beyond the limited boundaries of traditional notions of families and values.

This book contends that traditional conceptions of family must be rethought in light of the realities of contemporary American society. We argue that lesbian and gay family structures may serve a prophetic role in the redefining of familial relations. We present a sociological, political, and ethical critique of the concept of family, informed by a lesbian-gay perspective. We also provide a critical analysis of lesbian-gay families and engage debates within our own communities about marriage, children, kinship networks, and so forth. For example, we argue that, rather than simply mimicking heterosexual society, gay-lesbian families offer an alternative vision for all of society.

We do not pretend to represent all gay men or lesbians in the United States. We have a particular context out of which we write. We both hold Ph.D.'s in social ethics. We both have a background as Christians. One of us is an Episcopal priest, the other a university professor in a religious studies department. While we both have been troubled by elements within the Christian tradition, this is still part of our context and we make use of it (both critically and constructively) in our reflection in this book. We are also white, middle-class Americans. Both of us live and work in southern California. While we do not presume to speak for those of other class or racial/ethnic backgrounds, or for those who have other religious traditions or none at all, we have listened to other voices, both through the printed word and through dialoguing with others in our focus groups. Yet we must be clear that the perspective we present emerges from our context and is shaped by it. We encourage others to listen and respond from their contexts.

We have not conducted a social scientific study, although we have conducted focus groups and individual interviews so that we could listen to the perspectives of other lesbians and gay men and dialogue with them about family. We conducted four focus groups of between seven and nine people each to help us address the issues of family and family values. Focus groups help us assess people's ideas on particular issues with a minimum of interference from a researcher. Generally, members of the group begin to dialogue with each other. The researcher periodically will ask questions to start discussion of a particular area of interest. In our case, we asked subjects to discuss their biological family relationships, their understanding of gay friends as family, issues of coupling, issues concerning having children (for those who have or were considering having children), and the participants' understanding of family values.

Participants included gay men and lesbians, some in ongoing relationships with a partner and others who did not currently have such relationships. Some had children, others did not. A few were Hispanic; one was African American. All were middle-class and generally had high levels of education (at least an undergraduate degree). The names of the participants have been changed to protect their anonymity. Our work used these groups as a means of broadening our perspective on lesbian and gay families. This material was supplemented by individual interviews. We did not conduct a rigorous qualitative study in which focus groups provided the data for extensive analysis. Rather, our focus groups and interviews were useful in evoking ideas. Perhaps this study may provide a basis from which more rigorous empirical work might be developed.

Acknowledgments

This book was originally conceived as a paper presented to the American Academy of Religion in 1992. The process of developing this paper into a book has indebted the authors to many people whose contributions proved invaluable. In particular, we would like to thank Cynthia Eller and Linda A. Moody for their careful reading of several drafts and their constructive critiques along the way.

Mark wants to thank the parish of St. Wilfrid of York for encouragement and support during the process of writing this book. Elizabeth extends her thanks to California State University, Northridge, and the Department of Religious Studies for a sabbatical leave in which to finish the manuscript.

We also wish to thank the many people who shared their lives and experiences with us during interviews and focus groups, and who helped us think through ideas and questions about family values. We both wish especially to thank Steven Knise for his long-suffering support of our project, and of us, as we held focus groups, brainstormed over dinners, and wrote and rewrote drafts of the manuscript. We extend grateful thanks to Linda Jones, who prepared the final draft of the manuscript.

We also thank the staff at Pilgrim Press: Timothy G. Staveteig, our editor, for believing in the book; Kelley Baker, for her patience in answering our innumerable questions; and Ed Huddleston, for steering us through the copyediting and typesetting process.

I

Introduction: The Limits of Our Language

Several single-family homes line a street in the San Fernando Valley in southern California. Nothing seems remarkable about the well-trimmed lawns, the cars parked in the driveways, the children playing in the yards. Neighbors wave friendly greetings to one another as they go about the business of their lives.

To all appearances, this is the typical American neighborhood that has been celebrated in popular culture since the 1950s. And yet, this image has undergone change in the past forty years. An African American couple, husband and wife, live on this street with their four children; a white married couple live with their two toddlers. Perhaps it no longer surprises us that nuclear families of differing races live together on the same block, but there are other differences here that challenge the image of the American family.

This street is also home to two brothers, both gay, who live with a lesbian friend. An older gay couple lived on this street until recently. A few years ago one of the men died of cancer and the other died several months later; they had lived together for thirty-five years. A Hispanic lesbian lives next door to a couple of gay white men. A single straight woman lives a few doors down the block.

While this neighborhood may be more diverse than many across America, it is a real neighborhood in a not untypical U.S. city. This neighborhood provides an example of the diversity of families that live not only in the San Fernando Valley or in California but also across the United States. The standard image of the American family—husband, wife, two kids, and a dog—that inhabited the world of television comedies in the 1950s and 1960s is no longer the real world we live in and may not have even been as characteristic of earlier decades as we have been led to think.

We have witnessed relationships between people that neither fit the mold of the traditional nuclear family nor are "simply" friendships. What word can describe the commitment entered into by groups of friends who share the history of their lives? What word can describe the partnership of two women or two men as they fight to forge a life together, not only amid the pressures of daily life in the late-twentieth-century United States, but in a society where their lives and loves are invisible, where no language exists to fully and adequately name their reality?

Whose Family Values?

The idea of this book was first conceived during the 1992 presidential elections. As academics trained in the discipline of religious social ethics, we were troubled by the fact that, in public discourse, a single voice claimed to represent the religious perspective on the family. Advocates of the religious right became the champions of "family values."[1] Vice President Dan Quayle decried the morality of a fictional television character, Murphy Brown, because she symbolized what Quayle identified as a liberal attack on the family. Murphy Brown was a professional woman and single mother. What, exactly, were the family values she flouted? Quayle's critique centered on the importance of two-parent families and especially the presence of fathers in the home.

Politicians and leaders of the conservative right, however, often gave no content to this "family values" rhetoric. The term became political shorthand for a reassertion of the heterosexual, nuclear family, complete with traditional gender roles. Dad's place was in the world of work and public life, while Mom kept the home fires burning and infused the children with godly morality. What troubled us about this rhetoric was that it called for the dominance and legal privileging of this model to the exclusion of other forms of family and the diverse experiences of Americans who lived lives that did not match this norm.

We began writing this book to explore not only the different ways gay men and lesbians live as families, but also the values that emerge from these experiences. What, we wondered, would family values look like if not viewed through the lens of patriarchy and heterosexism? How might we construct family values from the perspective of gay men and lesbians? We spent some time reflecting on these questions and interviewing other lesbians and gay men, both couples and singles, about their perspectives on family values. The responses of these men and women appear in our book, although the names and identifying disclosures of participants have been changed to protect their anonymity.

The debate over the family and family values is only one battlefield in the greater culture war to define American life, but it is perhaps the most significant one. As sociologist James Davison Hunter has put it: "In many ways, the family is the most conspicuous field of conflict in the culture war. Some would argue that it is the most decisive battleground."[2] We do not have to look far to see the battle lines being drawn. In early 1996, the Supreme Court in Hawaii declared there is no constitutional ground on which to deny marriage rights to lesbians and gay men; whether this will hold up under appeal remains to be seen. In response, on September 10, 1996, in Washington, D.C., both the House and the Senate overwhelmingly passed the Defense of Marriage Act. This piece of legislation prohibits the federal government from recognizing same-sex marriages, and permits individual states to ignore such ceremonies performed in Hawaii or elsewhere. At the same time, organizations such as Promise Keepers are drawing thousands of men who are responding to the challenge to be better husbands and fathers, and to assume their God-given place as the head of the household. As Hunter observes, the fundamental issue in this war is over the definition of "family." If the American family is the microcosm of society, then defining it has decisive political implications.[3]

Defining the Family

In the battle over the family, can one word mean many things? Who does the defining? The most common definitions of family are reflected in dictionary definitions such as this one: "a set of parents and children or of relatives; a person's children."[4] This definition demonstrates the biological basis of our taken-for-granted notions of family. But the word "family" carries with it far more than this simple definition implies. As Nelle Morton explains: "Words do more than signify. They conjure images. . . . Images, therefore, are infinitely more powerful than concepts. Concepts can be learned . . . corrected . . . made precise . . . formulated, enclosed and controlled. . . . Images, on the other hand, cannot be so controlled."[5]

The word "family" conjures images shaped by individual and collective experiences, by the media, and by the cultural mystique of the family. The image of the family holds a mystique in American culture in much the same way that Betty Friedan described the "feminine mystique."[6] In her now-landmark book, Friedan identified a myth of femininity operating among middle-class women that masked the reality of their lives. In discussing the feminine mystique, Susan Faludi adds that women in the America of the 1950s, the era in which this mystique was perhaps most ardently advanced, did not match the image of stay-at-home moms. Rather, women were entering the workforce in large numbers. "It was precisely women's unrelenting influx into the job market," Faludi writes, "not a retreat to the home, that provoked and sustained the antifeminist furor."[7] A similar mystique of the "traditional family" renders invisible a large number of American families whose lives do not reflect that image. Furthermore, the recent furor concerning protection of the traditional family and family values disguises the fact that the American family is in fact changing.

Given all the confusion about the family, it did not surprise us to find conflicting opinions among the lesbians and gay men we interviewed for this book. Like most people in contemporary American society, the interviewees found themselves bound by traditional language and cultural images of the family, even as they struggled to identify their own relationships over and against it. When we asked a group of lesbian couples how they understood family, the following comments were made:

> "[Family] certainly doesn't mean anything we do; it's much more based on you have a daddy and a mommy and a car and a garage, and a pet . . ."

> "I grew up in a family, too, where the family thought that everyone sticks together and if somebody marries, that person becomes part of the family just because they got married."

> "The core family—that's not my experience. I felt always that I had to go outside of my family. I always felt the same—even when I was in college—and I was not identified as gay at that time. But I lived with these groups of kids, with girls, and I felt very strongly like I wanted to create the family I had found."

Within a group of single persons, both male and female, similar conflict about what constitutes the family emerged. Some of their reflections are as follows:

> "What does it mean to me? I know it doesn't mean two kids, a wife, a station wagon, and a dog. For me it means probably more like a group of

> friends. I'm in a special situation because my brother is [also] gay—the fact that we live together, that creates another family unit for us."
>
> "For me it becomes total acceptance of any situation in which there is love and caring, so that any grouping together, as long as that exists, becomes a family."
>
> "A family usually supports each other . . ."
>
> "Even though you know they don't want to call, family members call because that's what you do because you are family."
>
> "Sometimes blood is thicker than water, and I don't know whether or not they have to call one another; it's just something you do if you are in a family. If we choose the family we're there because we want to be there for each other and accept each other."

Even those who understand that they do not fit within the model of the traditional family struggle with traditional language and images as they explain their own lives. They must find a way to negotiate the territory of the traditional claims of family while mapping new territory outside its boundaries.

The nuclear, child-centered family has been called the "traditional family." If we understand tradition to mean that which existed in the past century or two, then this is a fair description. This image of family is also traditional in the sense that our modern understanding of the function of the family is not very different from that found throughout much of Western civilization; the family has been understood as the foundation of society. What goes unexamined, however, is the difference in notions of family that operated in earlier eras, and the social, economic, and political forces that effected changes in our understanding of family. In this regard, the "traditional" family is a relatively modern creation.

In sum, we believe that substantive definitions of the family, those that describe what family is by the characteristics of the members and their specific relation to each other (e.g., the nuclear family), are less useful and more restrictive than functional definitions that focus on the quality of relationship between persons and the function of those relations in the lives of family members. Thus, we propose a working definition of family: a committed relationship, developed over time, between persons who participate in each other's lives emotionally, spiritually, and materially. While this definition does not mention biology, it does not exclude it. Moreover, it is not a definition of what might already exist, but a vision of what family can be at its best. In this way, family itself is a value.

The Family and Ideology

The icon of the family functions ideologically in our society. Ideologies are composites of beliefs that shape the way we view the world. When an ideology functions in a society it appears to be the natural course of events, the way things are. An ideological construction says, "This is the way the world is." In actuality, however, the social arrangements the ideologies mask as natural are social constructions that are not given, but are produced by society. People are socialized to believe there are no other choices.[8]

"Commonsense" understandings of the traditional family are ideological constructions. For example, conservative religious leader Jerry Falwell defines the family as "the God-ordained institution of the marriage of one man and one woman together for a lifetime with their biological or adopted children."[9] For Falwell, heterosexual married couples with children form the essence of the family. The biological differences between men and women and the biological fact that heterosexual intercourse may result in offspring provide evidence to Falwell that the nuclear family is "natural" and ordained by God as right and proper. Conversely, all family relations that do not replicate this image are, in his view, inferior at best and sinful and unnatural at worst.

Heterosexuality is the "natural" paradigm for human sexual relations within this ideology, and women play a role in subordination to men. These views on gender relations within the family reflect a "commonsense" ideology about gender roles in society as a whole. Women, by virtue of their biological role as childbearers, have a "natural" role in the private sphere of the home. Men have a "natural" duty to take their place in the public sphere, in the world of work.

This "commonsense" understanding of the heterosexual family appears not only in the rhetoric of the right, but also in many social scientific treatments of the family. For example, Frances Goldsheider and Linda Waite make a distinction between "new families" and "no family."[10] The new families they discuss fit the structure of the nuclear family model characterized by bearing and raising children through the social institution of heterosexual marriage. They are distinguished from the traditional model, however, in that they are characterized by greater gender equality, with both partners sharing family responsibilities in the home and both working outside the home. While these authors mention other living arrangements, these are not considered family. Other possibilities, such as families formed by lesbians or gay men, remain invisible under the category of "no family."

Political theorist Susan Moller Okin examines gender and injustice in the family, but once again privileges the heterosexual model. Gay and lesbian families are dealt with in a cursory manner, in footnotes. Thus, she graphically marginalizes experiences that do not conform to the heterosexual norm.[11]

In an attempt to include a wider array of family forms in his definition of family, David Popenoe states: "I define the family as a relatively small domestic group of kin (or people in kin-like relationship) consisting of at least one adult and one dependent person."[12] While Popenoe attempts to provide a broader definition of family, unfortunately he makes dependence the defining characteristic of familial relationships. More precisely, he seems to imply that it is women's dependence on men and children's dependence on parents which defines family, since these are the traditional forms of hierarchical relationship. This is a definition long criticized by feminists.[13]

Furthermore, this definition does not cover heterosexual couples who are married, as well as gay or lesbian couples, in which both partners work and are independent. The definition becomes even more confusing when one considers the case of a gay couple in which both partners are independent. What if one partner became seriously ill with AIDS? Would this couple, previously not defined as family, now become a family due to the dependence of one partner on the other? This definition raises more questions than it answers.

Definitions of family such as these, which presume heterosexual marriage, the production and care of children, or the economic dependence of some members, exclude many of those we interviewed. Take, for example, the grouping of two lesbian couples: four adult women living together, without children present, all of whom are economically independent. According to the above definitions they are not family, yet they own a home together and clearly understand themselves to function as family for each other. One of these four women explained the relationship in the following way:

> "I think once we [all four] decided to live together, you know we were good friends to begin with, so we were more than just regular friends. The people that I have here are my family."

Some recent social scientific literature exploring broader definitions of family seems to support the redefinition of family expressed by these four women. For example, Carol Stack has studied African American kinship networks that often include both kin and non-kin relationships.[14] This experience caused Stack to rethink her understanding of family. The essays gathered by Barrie Thorne and Marilyn Yalom, in *Rethinking the Family: Some Feminist Questions,* examine a wide range of family experiences. The authors question traditional understandings of family from a feminist perspective.[15] Kath Weston has studied gay and lesbian kinship based on choice rather than biology.[16] These works represent a movement within social science research to broaden our understanding of family, based on a diversity of experiences.

Yet, the privileged place of "the family" is still ideologically dominant. Social institutions such as the media, religion, educational institutions, and government have been slow to acknowledge alternative family forms. Alternative discourse concerning the family, challenging the patriarchal model, has erupted in recent years and has resulted in our current cultural war over the family.

The Historical Construction of Family: The Power of a Myth

Contemporary defenders of traditional family values claim that a particular model of the family is normative, and has always been so. However, historical examination reveals that the modern understanding of the family as the nuclear, child-centered unit that serves as a refuge from society is a relatively recent development in Western society.

Modern concepts of family life are infused with romantic ideals about love, commitment, and emotional fulfillment that were not operative in earlier eras. Until recently the significance of the family was political in nature rather than a source of personal fulfillment. According to historian Gerda Lerner, "The archaic state, from its inception, recognized its dependence on the patriarchal family and equated the family's orderly functioning with order in the public domain."[17]

If we look back in history to the classical world of Greco-Roman culture, we find that marriage and family life were not the place where an individual's affective and intellectual needs were met; rather, the institution of marriage served to meet the material needs of the household and, by extension, the state. The Greek philosopher Aristotle, for example, argued that the family was a "necessary condition for, but not . . . an integral part of, the polis [the city-state]."[18] The city, he claimed, was by nature prior to the household, and to each individual, "for the whole must of necessity be prior to the part."[19] Since the household was defined as a part of the city, the family did not have intrinsic virtue; its virtue was defined in relation to the city, in the way in which it contributed to the good of the city.[20] Family life was an obligation one fulfilled for the good of the polis.

Furthermore, as historian Wayne Meeks points out, the meaning of family as household in the classical world is far broader than contemporary understandings of the nuclear family. "Family" is defined not first by kinship but by the relationship of dependence and subordination. The head of a substantial household was thus responsible for—and expected a degree of obedience from—not only his immediate family but also his slaves, former slaves who were now clients, hired laborers, and sometimes business associates or tenants.[21]

The emergence of Christianity did not drastically alter this model of household and family. Aristotle's view that the family functioned for the good of the state was echoed by Christian thinkers such as Augustine of Hippo.[22] In *The City of God* Augustine examines the relation of the family/household to the state, arguing that the use of all temporal things ought to be directed toward the achievement of earthly peace in the earthly city. By obeying the commands to love God and neighbor, peace would be attained, and this begins with the household. Why is domestic peace so important in God's scheme?[23] Augustine answers, "Now a man's house ought to be the beginning, or rather a small component part of the city. . . . Domestic peace contributes to the peace of the city . . . [because this] . . . contributes to the ordered harmony concerning authority and obedience obtaining among the citizens." Thus, a father should "govern his household in such a way that it fits in with the peace of the city."[24]

Augustine's thinking, then, provides a Christianized version of Aristotle. The family does not exist to provide for the meeting of individual needs, but rather as the foundation for society.

In addition, even before Augustine, Christian thinkers argued that celibacy, not marriage, was the ideal state of life. However, for those who could not live as celibates, marriage was preferred to concupiscence; in this sense marriage was thought to be a second-best choice. In his *Confessions,* Augustine recalls his desire to form a household composed of male friends:

> And many of us friends conferring about, and detesting the turbulent turmoils of human life, had debated and now almost resolved on living apart from business and the bustle of men; and this was to be thus obtained; we were to bring whatever we might severally procure, and make one household of all; so that through the truth of our friendship nothing should belong especially to any; but the whole thus derived from all, should as a whole belong to each, and all to all.[25]

In the end, the friends' dreams are confounded because of the obligation to marry. Clearly, however, marriage is a poor second choice for Augustine since spiritual pursuits are best accomplished in a community of friends. Nevertheless, the ideal of a celibate household of same-sex friends flourished as communities of "brothers" and "sisters" formed in monasteries and convents across Europe throughout the Middle Ages.

In the Middle Ages two themes from the classical period will be expanded and solidified: (1) that procreation is the primary purpose of marriage and (2) that marital monogamy is necessary for political stability. Jean-Louis Flandrin and Philippe Ariès, both historians of the family,[26] indicate that the Protestant Reformation in the sixteenth century and the response of the Roman Catholic Church to this were key in reshaping conceptions of the family. It is worthwhile, therefore, to examine the ideas of Martin Luther, the father of the Protestant Reformation, as they pertain to marriage and family. In the *Lectures on Genesis,* Luther declares the household to be instituted by God when God created Eve to be a wife for Adam. Luther draws a parallel between the establishment of domestic life and that of civil government, implying that both orders are ordained by God for the good of humanity. Luther poses the question, "When God says: 'It is not good that man should be alone,' of what good could he be speaking?" His answer is that "God is speaking of the common good or that of the species, not of personal good."[27]

Luther departs from previous ideas about marriage and family life. For him marriage is not a "necessary evil" but rather a divine commandment. Citing Genesis 1:28, where God tells Adam and Eve to "be fruitful and multiply," Luther asserts, "We may be assured that man and woman should and must come together in order to multiply."[28] According to Luther, it is within the family that Christian virtues will be learned and nurtured (a certain departure from Augustine's idea that marriage will distract one from spiritual pursuits). Luther extends the notion of vocation to parenting; bearing and raising children is described by Luther as a sacred calling. Married persons, Luther asserts, "can do no better work and do nothing more valuable either for God, for Christendom, for all the world, for themselves, and for their children than to bring up their children well."[29] According to Luther, marriage and family "is a divine kind of life."[30]

Both Flandrin and Ariès note a similar development in Roman Catholic teaching, with the privileging of the family as a place of Christian life. The family became the norm and the ideal where Christian virtues were taught and practiced. They also note that the emergence of the modern nuclear family structure corresponds to the privatization of society.

For most of the Middle Ages, the conditions of life did not allow for withdrawal of the household from the outside world. The image of the domestic family, akin to our modern concept, emerged near the end of the Middle Ages among the upper classes, because it is this group that had the financial means to withdraw into itself. Servants, clients, and friends were eventually excluded from definitions of family. This later image of family is characterized, according to Ariès, by the way in which it "cuts itself off from the world and opposes to society the isolated group of parents and children."[31] However, he also points out that this will continue to be limited to the wealthier classes for quite some time.

Debates about the role and function of the family continued in the Age of Enlightenment and must be understood within the context of the political ferment of the times. John Locke and other liberal thinkers sought to overturn paternalistic notions of government that supported the monarchy. They offered in its place a social contract model of government and described marriage in these new contractarian terms. According to Locke, the family was an agreement or compact between two individuals, a man and a woman. While Locke appears to uphold the equality of both marriage partners, he nevertheless maintains a traditional position regarding the subordination of wives. The husband has a "natural" duty to rule, as he is both abler and stronger, though Locke insists that he is to rule only in the common interests of the partners.[32]

This tendency of Enlightenment theory to describe the family as a "natural" institution enabled men like Jean-Jacques Rousseau to ignore the often oppressive relationships between husbands and their wives and children. According to political theorist Susan Moller Okin, Rousseau believed that "nature necessitates women's subjection to men, and the imperfections of men's nature necessitate the reinforcement of women's natural propensity for enduring injustice. The good of society and the continuation of the species make inevitable the rigid division of labor between the sexes and the subordination of women."[33]

We are the inheritors of such Enlightenment thought. If the family is "natural," it is beyond the scope of justice. Justice applies to the negotiation of competing rights in the public arena of enterprise and politics, and the privatization of the family theoretically removed it from that arena. However, there is a paradox in this. While the family is removed to the private realm, there remains the tendency to invest it with political meaning and significance. These contradictions will shape our understandings of the family in American society.

In her historical examination of families in America,[34] Stephanie Coontz[35] notes that it was after the Revolutionary War that the family began to develop into what is now identified as the traditional family. Its emergence must be understood as a response to changing economic and political realities. The Industrial Revolution provided new sources of income, facilitating the growth of a middle class. At the same time, the ideology of self-determination that fueled the Revolutionary War came to be promoted in the rhetoric of the American Dream, a view of the United States as a place where anyone could achieve anything through hard work and determination.

This ideology, however, presented a conflict when it came to gender roles, raising the question of how women's domestic subordination could be justified while still upholding a doctrine of equal rights for all. Post-Revolutionary rhetoric about women therefore focused on the idea that gender roles were the unavoidable result of "natural" differences between the sexes. Women were said to be naturally suited to the domestic sphere, and their most important political contribution was to raise patriotic children. Men, on the other hand, were thought naturally suited to work in the public sphere of politics and business. By remaining in their appropriate spheres, men and women served as complements to each other and created a divinely ordained balance in society.

Of course, this was a privileged ideal, for only the middle and upper classes had sufficient economic independence to permit women to remain at home and the family to be substantially independent of the community. The frequent disparity between ideology and the actual conditions of existence is especially glaring in the nineteenth-century ideology of family. While clergymen and politicians championed the nuclear family as the divinely sanctioned family model, the slave system during the antebellum period and the politics of racism that followed the Civil War would tear African American families apart. The rural and urban poor, both black and white, did not have the financial resources to enable women and children to retreat into the private home. In addition, in rural areas the distinctions between the private and public spheres of work did not make sense; family farms were the economic base of the family, and men and women shared the labor of the farm. Thus, among poor and working-class families the ideology of the nuclear family, self-sufficient and protected from the outside world, was unobtainable. Extended kinship ties and friendship networks were necessary for survival.

According to Coontz, by the twentieth century the family is identified as the principal source of individual fulfillment: "Not until the present century did nuclear families envision themselves as capable of meeting all the emotional needs of husband and wife and refusing interference from neighbors, same-sex networks, and other kin."[36]

This image of the family is central to the contemporary family mystique. Deviation from the familial norm has been considered suspect and even seditious. A study of schizophrenic women in the 1950s, for example, reports that women who did not embrace their domestic roles were sometimes defined as mentally ill and received electric shock therapy to help cure their "disorder."[37] During the same period homosexuality was thought to be as serious a threat to American society as communism (and in the McCarthy era the two were often held to be synonymous).

In the current debate about family values, these images of family that emerged from the nineteenth century onward shape our understanding of ourselves and our relationships, whether they include us or not.

The historical discussion we have advanced in this chapter is a necessary context in which to begin our discussion of alternative family values. Our intent is not to hearken back to some "golden age" of family, nor do we want to dismantle the family. Rather, it is our assertion that "family" is a cultural construction, one that has undergone multiple transformations without being destroyed. If it has survived changes in the past, surely it can do so again.

What we have said thus far raises further questions about the relation of family to community and the intersecting or overlapping roles these have played. An extended discussion of this issue will be developed in chapter 8. Here we simply note that there has been a consistent tendency to equate order and authority in the home with order and authority in the state. This will continue, to the present day, to legitimate a hierarchical, and often oppressive, family structure despite claims that the family provides a refuge and protection for its members. At the same time, modern understandings cast the family as a refuge from society, a privileged and protective enclave withdrawn into itself.

Important, then, to the lesbian and gay appropriation of "family" is the concern whether the family (middle-class and individualistic) is antithetical to the community (which has been so important to gay and lesbian survival). As Philippe Ariès notes, "One is tempted to conclude that sociability and the concept of the family were incompatible, and could develop only at each other's expense."[38]

The Scope of This Book

In discussing the scope of our work we need to discuss briefly what this book is not about. This is not a book on the history of the family, although we make use of history to place our contemporary setting in perspective. This is not a self-help book or a "how to" book for gay couples. This is not the story of a particular family or several families. We do not focus on the relationship between lesbians and gay men to their biological families, although we refer to these relationships. Other books address these issues and we refer to many of them in the course of our work.

In this book we explore the concept of family and family values from a lesbian and gay perspective. We place lesbian and gay men's family structures and same-sex couples at the center of our discussion rather than at the margins. This is not simply a methodological decision; it is a deliberately political one. According to social theorist and critic Gayatri Chakravorty Spivak, the dominant historical narrative always requires some persons to occupy the margins so that others may be defined as central to the narrative. In the history of family ideology, lesbians and gay men have occupied the margins, allowing the heterosexual norm to assert dominance. As a form of resistance, Spivak asserts that "the only strategic thing to do is to absolutely present oneself at the centre."[39]

We seek to consider the dynamics of family structures in terms of their impact on interpersonal relationships and social structures and systems. We locate the family in a discussion of personal and social ethics with an extended discussion of family values. Our discussion also involves a political critique of the family in the broader context of contemporary society in the United States. In particular we explore the political challenge that lesbian and gay families represent. As we see it, these alternative forms of family clearly challenge the privileged place of the nuclear family in law and society. At the same time, we wonder whether the increasing recognition of these family forms in our society may seduce gay men and lesbians into complacency. The challenge for lesbians and gay men is to continue thinking of ways in which our personal lives intersect the political, and how this intersection provides a critical position from which to work for a more just society.

We address the question of whether it is appropriate to use the word "families" for the structures of love and support developed by lesbians and gay men. In so doing, are we simply mimicking the heterosexual paradigm as the norm? Can we make a word mean so many things? Should we even want to do so? We believe that a renewed understanding of the family is an appropriate starting point for gay men and lesbians to explore their relationships and the political meaning these hold for society as well as for lesbian and gay communities. We hope to add our voice to a dialogue that will result in making the family a sphere of love and justice.

Part I

Finding a Grammar for Family Values

Fidelity

The mystique surrounding traditional family values provides comfort to some as a source of stability in the face of unsettling social change. Others argue that the focus on family values leaves large segments of society marginalized and invisible at best, and masks an agenda of discrimination and hate toward minority communities at worst. Despite the highly charged and emotional rhetoric of our current culture war over the family, few spokespersons on either the right or the left have clearly articulated or defined the values at stake.

Societal values often remain an unspoken part of the taken-for-granted reality of everyday life. The very fact that family values and the nature of family itself have become the source of political and societal debate in our time demonstrates that traditional understandings have lost their "naturalness" and their fluency in public discourse. In this and the following chapters we discuss values that emerge from family life as it has been traditionally defined and that create the mystique of family. The many women and men we interviewed helped us in our attempt to clarify, interpret, and even name the values we discuss.

While there is much that can be celebrated in the traditional values surrounding family relations, there is also much that we can learn from the experiences and perspectives of those who do not fit the traditional family model. As lesbians and gay men, we live our lives often within two worlds, one in which we share the meanings and values of the biological family and a second in which we re-create family with our partners, friends, and—sometimes—children. In bridging these two worlds we bring much that is valuable from our enculturation in the biological family to the families we create. Sometimes our dreams go unrealized; often our expectations are unrealistic. Nevertheless, the values surrounding the traditional home and family are often our values too. Thus, while we critique traditional values, particularly as they have been a source of oppression, we also affirm the values of committed relationship and reinvest them with meanings that have a better fit with our lives.

Faithfulness to a Committed Relationship

Ed and Roger lived in a suburban neighborhood for most of their more than thirty years as partners. A few years ago Roger was diagnosed with lung cancer. During his long battle with his illness, Ed stood by Roger's side. When he became too weak to get around on his own, Ed would help feed and bathe Roger and help him get dressed. During this same time Ed's ninety-three-year-old mother, who had lived in an apartment attached to Ed and Roger's home, had to move to a convalescent facility because she required a level of care Ed could not provide. She died not long after. A few months later Roger left home to go to the hospital and never came back. Not long after Roger's death, Ed was also diagnosed with lung cancer. As he became more frail, Hugo, a young man whom Ed knew, moved in with him and took charge of his care. Soon afterwards Hugo's boyfriend, Enrique, also moved in. When Ed died from the disease as well, Hugo and Enrique continued to live in the house until Ed's relatives, and a lesbian the men had known for many years, could arrange to sell the property. Before they moved, however, the two men decided they wanted to affirm their relationship in a marriage ceremony. The day of the event, their biological family and their friends gathered to celebrate the love to which these two committed themselves.

The value of fidelity, faithfulness to a committed relationship, is central to the discussion of family values. As the preceding story demonstrates, fidelity is not the exclusive territory of religious or political conservatives. Our discussion and critique of fidelity should not therefore be seen as a rejection of the value of fidelity, but rather as our attempt to explore why fidelity is important to the concept of family and to expand the parameters within which we understand both family and fidelity.

The concept of fidelity as a family value tends to be narrowly construed in common understandings, focusing essentially on married partners. The talk-show circuit abounds with programs that focus on "men who cheat on their wives" and "women who have affairs," but these same shows do not explore the topic of "children who cheat on their parents" or "parents who are unfaithful to their children." This is not to say that such programs have not discussed parents and children who have betrayed each other's trust, but these are not framed within the language of fidelity. Within the traditional paradigm, fidelity or faithfulness has come to be equated with sexual monogamy in heterosexual marriage.[1]

Lesbians and gay men are often perceived as a threat to the family because it is believed that we are more sexually promiscuous than heterosexuals, and less able to maintain long-term relationships. Clearly, however, sexual fidelity is a problem within the heterosexual community, and many are raising questions about the value of monogamy. It is no surprise, then, that we find similar questions being raised by gay men and lesbians. In our interviews, the issue of monogamy within relationships frequently came up, and both men and women struggled with this. In a focus group with lesbian couples, one woman discussed the difficulties posed by having sex outside the primary relationship:

> "I think it would be easy for me to find somebody I like that I want to sleep with; but then I'd have to come home and tell her, and there's too much pain. Forget about it. Too much trouble. The talks you'd have to have for one stupid night, forget about it."

Another woman responded:

> "I feel similarly. Intellectually I don't see any problem with the notion of having sex with someone else. It seems silly not to have that access. But I don't think it works for me. I would start worrying about it, so I would start poisoning myself with all of this stuff."

The first woman responded saying:

> "The other thing for me is that my partner trusts me, so if I'm going to sleep with somebody I have to tell her because we have these rules. I would have to tell her first; I feel like otherwise I would be betraying her because we have this agreement that is spoken or unspoken; it's an agreement. For me, if I would like to sleep with somebody else or have fun sexually, I would include her and we would all know and have fun."

In this conversation all the women seemed to agree, on an intellectual level, that sexual acts outside their primary relationships were within the realm of possibility, although they also found that in their particular situations non-monogamy carried too high a price.

Others we interviewed, however, adhered to a more traditional understanding. For example, a single gay man affirmed his desire to be in a committed monogamous relationship:

> "I'm having a really hard time finding a relationship. I'm single and I really hate it, but I just haven't found the right person. I don't want to be with

> just anybody. It's got to be somebody with whom I can create the bond that I didn't have. What I want as a family is to have a spouse, not children, but someone you can share your life with."

A little bit later in the conversation he returned to this theme:

> "I'm not one of these people who are into open relationships—for me that wouldn't constitute a family. You get married. You stay together. You work your problems out."

A focus group of single gay men and lesbians acknowledged that their attitudes about sexuality and monogamy were shaped in part by the values they learned in their families of origin. As one man put it:

> "My mother was one of those people who said, 'This is a family. Even though I may hate your father, you don't get divorced.' It's not something you do. I wasn't brought up that way."

What became clear to us, as we listened to numerous lesbians and gay men discuss the question of monogamy and sexual fidelity, was that there seemed to be as many varied opinions in our own communities as are found in the heterosexual world. There was no common agreement on whether fidelity for its own sake was a value that should be maintained.

Fidelity as Larger Than the Sexual Act

A story told in the focus group of lesbian couples illustrates that sexual fidelity is valued as symbolic of something larger than the sexual act itself. Sandy, a middle-aged professional woman, told us that she had lived with a woman for two years, feeling that over this time they had developed a relationship of trust and sexual fidelity. Then she found out that her partner had lied to her and had not been monogamous. Soon after this the relationship broke up. When Sandy started dating her present partner, Alicia, she still felt wounded. She could not establish a new relationship of trust because of the sense of betrayal she felt from her previous partner.

Even though sexual exclusivity is an element in this story, it certainly is not the central value violated by Sandy's first partner. Rather, it was the lack of honesty and the breach of trust that damaged the relationship. In this case, sexual acts were symbolic of a deeper breach within the relationship. Thus, fidelity implies a broader understanding of faithfulness and trust based on a history of lived experience with another. As Sandy explained, her earlier experience of betrayal has caused her to evaluate her actions in her present relationship very carefully:

> "I think one of the things that's different with us is because I am coming out of this relationship of betrayal. We have had this evolving dialogue about this issue in our relationship because we both came to say, 'Sooner or later you are going to be attracted to somebody else.' It's not natural to think that isn't going to happen, and sooner or later you are probably going to want to act on it. I think you can make decisions not to, but because of my experience I look at it and I don't want to be in denial and decide, 'Okay, honey, it's you and me the rest of our lives' and we will never be attracted to another person and never want to act on it.
>
> "Through the course of our relationship I have become infatuated with a number of different people—and I always return to my true love and my soul mate. So now we have evolved to a point where the relationship is primary and primary means this is where the energy begins and returns to and this is the place where we always have to be making sure that we are connected, that our sex life is hot, those things are in place in our relationship. As long as those things are in place, then whatever things might happen hopefully we will be able to deal with."

In light of these conversations, it seems to us that the value of fidelity needs to be expanded beyond the question of sexual monogamy. This is not to say that sexual fidelity between partners is not a value worth embracing. Neither, however, is it one that can be made an absolute. As our interviews revealed, faithfulness in relationship was considered important, and sexuality was simply one arena in which fidelity could be expressed. What might fidelity mean beyond this narrow understanding, and why might it be important as a family value? What would it mean for a child to be faithful to his/her family? What about fidelity for those who are unpartnered?

For lesbians and gay men, the understanding of fidelity as a family value must be broadened. We gay men and lesbians are all too often defined simply in terms of our sexual acts, and denigrated for this. Reduced to only our sexual selves, we are then told that these selves are what make us immoral. Even if we are sexually monogamous in our relationships, we are told that we do not have "values." If fidelity is a family value, how can we live this out in our lives? Why should we want to?

Theologian Jim Cotter states: "To be 'faithful' is to be 'full of faith,' full of trust, to be willing to let love be vulnerable. Only so can love create love, can the commitment be creative."[2] This understanding of fidelity is not focused on the sexual act, but on the total context of the relationship between persons who trust and love each other. Fidelity in this broader sense relates to promise keeping. Faithfulness exists in our relationships to the extent that others have made promises to us, and we trust their word, and they act in ways deserving our continued faith. In like manner, we make promises to others who have faith in us.

Ethicist Sissela Bok talks about the "principle of veracity," our trust in what others tell us, as a foundational principle for an ongoing relationship. Bok writes:

> I can have different kinds of trust: that you will treat me fairly, that you will have my interests at heart, that you will do me no harm. But if I do not trust your word, can I have genuine trust in the first three? If there is no confidence in the trustfulness of others, is there any way to assess their fairness, their intentions to help or to harm? How then can they be trusted? Whatever matters to human beings, trust is the atmosphere in which it thrives.[3]

In this understanding, fidelity relies on the congruence between the commitments we hold to others either explicitly stated or implicit, and the living out of those commitments. As Bok makes clear, a faithfulness, a truthfulness must exist between what we say and what we do. In fact, the commitments we have to others are first experienced through actions over time before they are voiced. When there is a history of experience, the words give voice to this. For example, in the modern marriage ceremony, husband and wife say "I do" in response to a series of promises based on a history in which they have come to trust in each other.

This broader understanding of the value of fidelity decenters sexual monogamy as a value in itself. Sexual expression between partners can be a symbolic expression of fidelity and of the uniqueness of a particular relationship. But it could also be an expression of violence or of one partner's domination of the other rather than a symbolic representation of love and trust.

We can imagine, for example, a situation in which a woman remains sexually faithful to a man out of fear that he will kill her if she does not.

In other words, the acts of sexual exclusivity in and of themselves cannot be immediately interpreted as "fidelity." Rather, sexual acts take on meaning in the context of the whole relationship between the partners. The entire loving relationship is reinforced by continued concrete expressions of love on a daily basis. This, in fact, is what it means to "make love."

Covenantal Relations

The biblical image of covenant can illuminate our understanding of fidelity. For the prophet Hosea, for example, faithfulness is tied to remembrance. Hosea recalls a history of relationship demonstrated through concrete experiences of love expressed over time between Israel and God. Conversely, faithlessness and forgetfulness are deemed sinful because they deny what has taken place between people and between people and God.

Hosea also makes clear that Israel cannot satisfy God simply by the performance of ritual acts: "For I desire steadfast love and not sacrifice, the knowledge of God rather than burnt offerings" (Hosea 6:6). Here Hosea echoes the words of other biblical prophets who reminded Israel that the covenant with God required more than mere legalistic adherence to formal codes of behavior. The prophet Amos, speaking for God, declares:

> "I hate, I despise your festivals, and I take no delight in your solemn assemblies. Even though you offer me your burnt offerings and grain offerings, I will not accept them; and the offerings of well-being of your fatted animals I will not look upon. Take away from me the noise of your songs; I will not listen to the melody of your harps. But let justice roll down like waters, and righteousness like an everflowing stream." (Amos 5:21–24)

Similarly, the prophet Micah declares that what God requires is that Israel "do justice," "love kindness," and "walk humbly with your God" (Micah 6:8).

The biblical model of covenant is a relational model. In all instances God requires faithfulness over time, not the performance of specific acts. No single act, in and of itself, can fulfill the covenant. Likewise, no particular act of unfaithfulness is irredeemable. In this understanding of fidelity, relationships are forged over time through acts where love is made incarnate. In turn, loving actions reinforce the significance of those relationships for us.

In addition, the covenantal model does not rely on the exercise of rational choice for participation in relationship, though it certainly does not exclude this either. For example, the covenant made with Israel did not include just adult males, though they were the only ones who could legally enter into contractual arrangements. The covenant was made with a people, including women, children, and slaves, who did not have legal standing in their own right. Thus, a covenantal model of fidelity is more inclusive than a contract; it provides a model whereby all members of the family may be exhorted to faithfulness.

In the absence of biological relationships or legally sanctioned unions, the cement that has joined families in more traditional definitions, covenantal relationship might be seen as the "tie that binds" members of chosen families. Fidelity in this case would only secondarily refer to sexual relations. Covenantal fidelity refers to the whole spectrum of responsibilities entailed in caring for and respecting those others to whom we are bound.

A broader understanding of fidelity in relationship does not define a priori the content of what faithfulness means. Rather, in covenantal relationships, persons agree, through words and deeds, to be *for* each other. They do not define in advance all the rules of the game. Being faithful is not simply performing duties, fulfilling one's part of the bargain. We draw a distinction between an ethic of duty and an ethic of love.

Duty alone, as the motivation for fulfilling commitments to others, fits well into a contract model of fidelity, while love finds congruence with a covenantal model. Duty may be comfortable because we know what is required of us; if we fulfill our obligations then we are faithful. Love, while it does not ignore responsibilities to others, is open-ended. Because we have a relationship with the other over time, we say yes to a future with them. We may not always be able to define what that future will be, or stipulate fully the boundaries of our commitment, but that is the adventure of the frontier that love opens to us.

A story told by Allan, a single gay man, helps clarify this understanding. At some point in his relationship with a lifelong friend, there was a falling out between them over "a stupid little thing." As a result, their friendship had become strained. And yet, as Allan continued to talk about it, it was clear that he had not given up on this relationship.

> "I said everything I needed to say to him when we were breaking up our relationship because I knew I could. We were teenagers together; there's nothing I can't say to him even if it's mean and nasty and angry. I can express all of my emotions with this friend who's really part family. If he ever needed something and called me I would be there for him in a minute and I think he would do the same for me if I really needed him. He would be there."

We might define fidelity therefore as a commitment to the struggle to love those with whom we are in relationship. In his book *Postmodern Ethics,* social theorist Zygmunt Bauman states that love requires us to move between the two dangers of "fixing" and "floating."[4] Fixing is attempting to ensure the continued presence of the other's care, concern, and responsibility. By the same token, fixing allows us to know our obligations and perform them, giving no more or less than what is demanded. Fixing is the security that is sought within a contract.

Floating involves "cutting one's losses," giving up when the costs of our investment in the relationship seem to have exceeded the return.[5] In this sense, floating is an economic model operating out of a contract understanding. If we understand faithfulness as committing to the struggle of love and avoiding these two dangers, then faithfulness involves commitment to relationship based on what we have shared in the past, but also an openness to the future that defies simple definition of obligations.

This broader, covenantal understanding of fidelity as trust based on shared history can characterize not only relations between partners but other familial relations as well, relationships that do not involve sexual expression. Thus it enables us to explore the importance of faithfulness as a family value as it extends to all members of the family. Kevin, a gay man in his thirties who lives with his brother Nathan, also a gay man, talked about the relationship he has with his father:

> "I hate my father at points, but yet that wouldn't stop me next time from—I mean, last year we had a real blowout fight, but next time when we're together it's like, he's my father and there's a history there, but again I wouldn't *not* hug him or kiss him."

Nathan, Kevin's brother, added that even though neither he nor Kevin currently was involved in a romantic relationship, their bond as brothers was characterized by faithfulness to each other wrought in the day-to-day experience of living together over time.

In response, Hannah, a lesbian in her forties, reflected on the idea that fidelity and trust are formed through a shared history:

> "I think about what you said about that bond. To me it's the length of time and intensity of the relationship, because I have two, maybe three ex-lovers that I feel are really part of my family. But that's because we've known each other for fifteen to twenty years. And the relationship when we were lovers or friends was fairly intense or inclusive. And my siblings too—we share a lot of history together that I don't share with anybody else and we have talked about this between ourselves. It's hard to share some of those things with other people."

Hannah noted that the bonds she shared with her siblings were forged in their shared experiences, experiences that no one else shared with her. At the same time, she felt bonds of faithfulness and trust with women she was no longer romantically involved with, but who remained in her life as part of her chosen family.

As seen through the interviews we conducted, gay and lesbian families of choice embrace the broader value of covenantal fidelity to include relations with other members of our gay/lesbian families. These too are created over time. Our history with one another continues to build our relationships and reinforces the commitment that already exists. In expanding a notion of fidelity to our close relationships beyond our primary partners, we need to explore faithfulness among friends.

Families and Friends

There is a clear distinction in American society between friends and family. Biological family ties are assumed to be enduring whereas relationships with friends are more ephemeral. In everyday language, distinctions are made between those friendships that are close and enduring and those that are more transitory, or between close friends and acquaintances. Yet the primary distinction upholds relationships of blood over those of friendship. As the saying goes, "Blood is thicker than water." In her study of friendship in American society, sociologist Lillian Rubin remarks that while our language gives us relatively few words to discuss friendship, there is a rich selection of terms available for describing biological relationships.[6]

Rubin notes that relationships with one's biological family are important in that these relationships help to give us a sense of our identity. Beyond these relationships, however, she discusses the importance of friendship:

> Whether child or adult, it is friends who provide a reference outside the family against which to measure and judge ourselves; who help us during passages that require our separation and individuation; who support as we adapt to new roles and new rules; who heal the hurts and make good the deficits of other relationships in our lives; who offer the place and encouragement for the development of parts of self that for whatever reasons are inaccessible in the family context. It's with friends that we test our sense of self-in-the-world, that our often inchoate, intuitive, unarticulated vision of the possibilities of a self-yet-to-become finds expression.[7]

Rubin's analysis relates to our understanding of fidelity in that the quality of relations with biological family members has less to do with our genetic links to them than with our shared history at formative times in our lives.

What is striking about Rubin's discussion of the importance of friends is her view that friendship serves to help formulate elements of ourselves that cannot be developed within our biological families. This is especially true for gay men and lesbians. Coming out is an experience often assisted by friends rather than family. Indeed, the experiences shared with friends help to transform our understanding of self as lesbian or gay. These relationships, forged over time, can be as significant as relationships with biological family, or more so. Given the significance of these relationships, our family of friends deserve our ongoing fidelity at least as much as our biological families do.

Here, again, a biblical understanding of covenant between friends reinforces this notion of fidelity. The story of the friendship between Ruth and Naomi illustrates this well. A Hebrew woman, Naomi, marries Elimelech and bears him two sons. A famine in Bethlehem causes the family to leave their home and go to the country of Moab, where Elimelech dies, leaving Naomi to raise her two sons alone in a foreign land. The sons grow up and marry two Moabite women, Ruth and Orpah. Then Naomi's sons die and she decides to return to Bethlehem, instructing her daughters-in-law to return to their own families. Orpah returns home, but Ruth tells her mother-in-law: "Do not press me to leave you or to turn back from following you! Where you go, I will go; where you lodge, I will lodge; your people shall be my people, and your God my God. Where you die, I will die—there will I be buried" (Ruth 1:16–17a).

Though this passage is often read as a part of traditional Christian wedding ceremonies, this was a promise made between two women, related by marriage but also by friendship. As feminist theologian Linda A. Moody points out, this covenant alters "the usual boundaries of familial and cultural allegiance," and represents a lifelong commitment on the part of these two friends.[8]

In our society there are no rituals or ceremonies celebrating friendship, nor are there the same social norms against distancing ourselves from friends as exist against separating ourselves from family members. While gay men and lesbians often value their friends as family, they cannot rely on the broader society for support for their relationships. Nor can the norms of society, which honor legalized marriage and biological families, govern their relationships with their chosen family. We believe that fidelity, as we describe it, can and should be valued among families of friends as among biological families.

While fidelity involves living out over time what we say our relationships mean, fidelity may also involve a spatial dimension. The mobility of contemporary society has often served to erode family relationships. Nuclear families have experienced isolation socially and geographically to a larger degree than have past generations, who relied on the social support of extended family networks.[9] This phenomenon was noted by a woman in one of our focus groups. Her family, she recounted, had moved away from an extended family. As a result, her family developed relationships with friends who lived nearby. These friends became a sort of second family. They would spend holidays together and act as a source of social support.

The sense of separation from biological nuclear families and extended kin networks is more acute for gay men and lesbians than it is for nuclear families. Whereas movement away from biological kin is often the result of economic motivations for traditional nuclear families, lesbians and gay men often move to get away from the confining atmosphere of their families and their communities. Moving away from biological kin may be a symbolic expression of the emotional isolation from their families that gay men and lesbians feel. Moving to a new city is often experienced as both leaving an old identity behind and creating a new self and an alternative family of friends in a new place. John Preston, in discussing the hometowns gay men leave and the new ones they embrace, notes that in the early days of gay liberation a gay man "could assume a new identity by becoming a member of a new clan." Yet becoming a member of the new clan "meant adopting the new hometown to the exclusion of the old."[10]

In his novel *Buddies,* Ethan Mordden tells the story of Ripley Smith, who leaves his hometown in South Dakota and moves to Manhattan, where he gets a new name, Carlo. As the story progresses Carlo leaves New York to return to his biological family. In a letter he writes to Bud, a member of his gay family back in Manhattan, he tells about reflecting on his gay family with an old friend from South Dakota, now married and a father. When the friend asked Carlo how he could live without a family, "I said my family is all the guys I was telling him about. Isn't it?" Carlo writes. "But he didn't get that. He said no—a family like playing with them and learning from each other and living with them inseparable, and I said that's what we do. And finally he sort of got it, that my family is my buddies."[11] In the end, Carlo returns to his gay family in New York realizing that he no longer feels at home in his old hometown. Carlo returns to the family to which he has chosen to be faithful, the family in which his identity had been created.

The story of Carlo and his gay family represents the alternative model of fidelity we articulate. Families of choice, families of friends, forge relationships with each other over time and out of their shared experience of exclusion from mainstream culture. In helping us give birth to new identities, gain new senses of self, our families of choice take on significance for us.

While the understanding of fidelity we have set forth does not exclude sexual monogamy, neither is it limited to nor defined by this. As we have noted throughout this chapter, lesbians and gay men have found it necessary to negotiate the territory between our biological families and our families of choice. Our values are often shaped by and are at the same time reactions against the values of the traditional family. Thus, while we continue to uphold fidelity as central to any understanding of family, we have found it necessary to expand the dimensions of both family and fidelity in order to be faithful to our own experiences.

3

Mutuality and Accountability

•→ Patty sits in her office in southern Arizona. Books line the shelves, and her desk is covered with papers. A college professor in her mid-forties, Patty laughs easily as we talk. When I ask her about her family's response to her lesbianism, and her current relationship with them, however, her face grows sad. "My dad died when I was nine. Mom raised my brother and me, with the help of caring grandparents. Though we had our differences, I counted on the support of my mother and, at too young an age, helped her survive a life-threatening marriage to her second husband. When I came out to my mother, it was awful. For five years, more or less, we had little conversation. One time when I went home, I tried to talk to her. Both of us became angry. I was devastated when she said in anger, 'Sometimes I wish you were dead.' And then, 'Sometimes I want to shoot you.' The story does not end there. Both of us have grown up a little. Now we can laugh together again. Though she is still uncomfortable about my being a lesbian and I have to censor my words and behavior, she laughs with my partner too."

A Sense of Obligation

One of the family values the men and women we interviewed struggled to name was the sense of obligation we feel toward members of our families, both biological and chosen. Within all the focus groups there was agreement that, when we commit ourselves to others in a covenant of familial relationship, we take on responsibilities to those others. Nevertheless, there was also the common experience that families often place undue expectations on family members.

For many persons, both gay and straight, the tension between the responsibility we feel toward our families and the obligations these families impose upon us is a source of conflict. While we recognize that those to whom we are committed may rightfully place expectations on us, often these expectations require a degree of self-sacrifice that seems unreasonable. For lesbians and gay men in particular, the demands of biological families often require a denial of self that is impossible to maintain while still retaining our dignity as persons. Thus, although those we interviewed clearly understood that the concept of family included obligations to one another, they wrestled with how to define these in ways that did not feel abusive or exploitative.

One of the interesting family groups we interviewed was a group of four lesbians, two couples who had chosen to make a home and family together. When we asked them to reflect on what sorts of obligations they felt toward each other, one of the women responded:

> "I think the meaning of obligation in families is there are certain places that you are required to be, you're expected to be, you go there whether or not it's organic to you, whether or not it's something you desire—you're obligated to do it. I think one of the things we struggle with in our group is how not to act out of obligation. It's like I wouldn't use that word. We have an obligation not to act out of that kind of obligation to one another."

The women in this particular group went on to differentiate between (1) obligation, as defined above; (2) duties, consisting of things one has committed to do for others; and (3) responsibilities, those things done for others out of care and concern for them. These are three senses in which commitment might be described. The first sense, obligation, was understood negatively. Yet duties and responsibilities still operated in their lives as a family of friends.

Unconditional Love

The understanding that our family members can expect a degree of commitment from us that others cannot is an extension of one of the greatest expectations that we place on our families: that they will love us unconditionally. One of the single gay men we interviewed said that, within his family of origin,

> "there is an understanding that 'they are always there' and you always have to love them, but there are definitely moments in which you don't."

Another single man in the group agreed:

> "I am in the same situation. I have a lesbian sister and what you just said reminded me of what my mother always said: 'I don't always like you kids, but I always love you' because there are always going to be struggles and differences, but that respect and unconditional love is always there."

The promise that the family will provide unconditional love and acceptance is perhaps one of the most seductive aspects of the family mystique. James B. Nelson describes it well:

> Each of us needs a place where the gifts of life make us more human, where we are linked with ongoing covenants to others, where we can return to lick our wounds, where we can take our shoes off, and where we know that—within the bounds of human capacity—we are loved simply because we *are*.[1]

For those of us raised on the TV shows of the 1950s, there is a tremendous nostalgic appeal in this image of unconditional acceptance. No matter how many times Bud or Cathy or Kitten screwed up (and they did some really stupid things, if memory serves correctly), *Father Knows Best* always ended with a warm and affirming picture of the solidarity of the family unit. One cannot imagine Ward and June Cleaver ever saying to the Beaver, "I wish you'd never been born!" or threatening to throw Wally out when he turned eighteen. Although today's TV shows may be more willing to admit that there are problems within the family, we also cling to these idealized visions of the family as a safe haven.

It is, however, more than just nostalgia that seemed to motivate the conversations of the men and women we interviewed. Despite acknowledging disappointments with their own families, there was also often a deeply felt longing for the family image that they had been brought up with.

As one critic of the idealized traditional family has argued, the family's main function is sentimental: "It serves as haven and oasis, emotional stabilizer and battery charger for its members. It demands that spouses and children love and trust one another, that they intensely enjoy being together."[2] This romanticized view presents such familial relationships as a "law of nature" rather than a consciously chosen commitment to other persons.[3] In this version of the family, unconditional love simply happens because we are bound by blood ties.

Presumed Duties and Obligations

The promised gift of unconditional love which our families offer to us carries with it the reciprocal requirement that we fulfill our obligations to the family. This is well represented in the hackneyed saying "Blood is thicker than water." On the one hand, this expression suggests unquestioned support from one's family members, no matter what. This kind of support often provides a sense of security. Nathan and Kevin, two gay brothers, affirmed the importance of such support in their own family of origin. Nathan discussed his mother's reaction to having two gay sons:

> "We never discussed my homosexuality. I found out that she knew; she acknowledged it with my older brother when she found out about Kevin. She called my older brother and said, 'I could understand one son, but now two?' There are only three of us, so she knew. Again, that type of thing that, yeah, you can always talk about it—yet we never have—and the idea that nothing is ever so bad that you can't talk about it. Even at points when she's fought with her own siblings, and there have been disagreements, it's always been, 'Well, I'll get over it in a while.' And she constantly pushes us, 'You guys can't ever fight; don't ever let things come between you.' "

At the same time, traditional definitions of familial love also require absolute prior loyalty to blood kin over and above all other relationships one may have. Kevin and Nathan acknowledged that, along with the security their family provided, they sometimes found it difficult to balance this against claims made by other relationships:

> "Like holidays for us, we're obligated. We don't go to friends, we don't go away, we don't go to Florida; we go to New Jersey—that's what you do. You don't even think about making plans to go anywhere else.

> "Our friends call our parents for permission—when we go home—to go to their house. They're saying, 'We're going to schedule a party on Sunday night; will Kevin and Nathan be allowed to come on Sunday night?' I'm thirty-three years old—I'm asking my parents permission to go out?!! Wait a minute!"

This pairing of unconditional love and duty/obligation is taken for granted in traditional understandings of the family, as our interviews demonstrate. Often our families of origin manage to fulfill their promise. Allan, a single gay man, explained that even though his family often struggled with their commitment to one another, they nevertheless managed to hold together. The lessons learned within his family of origin, which included "being there for each other—having people around who support you," are values he attempts to recreate in his own chosen family of friends.

Familial love, as many lesbians and gay men have discovered, however, may indeed be conditional. It can be, and often is, withdrawn if one does not fulfill the obligations of the dutiful daughter or son, and these obligations are more often than not constructed around a heterosexual norm. The son or daughter who chooses an option other than heterosexuality may be accused of destroying the family. As Kath Weston observed in her book *Families We Choose,* "Coming out to a biological relative puts to the test the unconditional love and enduring solidarity commonly understood in the United States to characterize blood ties."[4]

The men and women in our focus groups acknowledged that this was a test many families failed. A group of single lesbians and gay men talked about their own experiences, and those of others they knew:

> "My biological family accepts me, but for a long time they didn't know. So there was a little period of time after I came out where I wasn't sure if they were still going to accept me or not, and obviously we know a lot of people's families don't accept them. Hate is not a family value, but I think a lot of people learn hate as a family value. We hate people who are different than we are."

Another person responded:

> "Or fear—you fear the things that are not like you. In my family growing up, my father was very bigoted. I was different, so I got a lot of flak from

> him; consequently, anybody who is different is okay with me. That is a value I learned as opposed to a value that was taught."

In another group, Jenny, a single bisexual woman, discussed her own difficulty in coming out to her family:

> "I'm out to my mother and that's it, officially. I think my sister-in-law knows, which means my brother might know. I came out probably in the worst way; I sent them a letter, but I had tried like three times when I was home and I just couldn't do it. So I sent them a letter. Seven A.M. the phone rings and, unfortunately, my partner answered it, hands it to me, and my mother is just hysterical. My dad never saw the letter. She cried a lot, and has still not told my father because it would give him a heart attack. I'm not out to my other sister or brother. I was with my partner for seven years and just nothing! Like how do they not see just still amazes me!"

As these conversations reveal, the love that we are promised may be conditional upon our obedience and conformity to traditional family norms. Alicia, whom we interviewed in a group of lesbian couples, explained that her coming out was perceived as a choice against her biological family:

> "Well, unfortunately, my family had a real hard time with my coming out; in fact, we didn't go over for Christmas or that kind of thing because it was like, 'Okay, she's out. She's given up the family for this little woman.' My mother was always really supportive. In terms of my father, well, he died—he would have been a tough one. But my sister shares his legacy, and my brother. It has been ten years and they have never come to visit."

As Alicia experienced it, love was based on conforming to a traditional family model.

Obligation as Self-Sacrifice

Social ethicist Beverly Harrison has pointed out that twentieth-century Protestant theological ethics is characterized by a "pervasive emphasis on obedience to God," an emphasis that more often than not fails to specify in concrete terms the content of the requirement: obedience has become "not merely a free-floating but an empty category."[5]

Thus, obedience for its own sake is identified as a mode of moral action. Harrison goes on to state that "obedience-oriented approaches to action also have a strong tendency to convey the implication that 'good' action is a mode of 'doing for' others."[6] The family member who is "disobedient," who does not conform to familial expectations, runs the risk of being accused of not fulfilling the demands of unconditional love. "If you loved us," the transgressor may hear, "you would not do this thing." The notion of obedience, then, carries with it, at least implicitly, the demand for self-sacrifice.

Harrison asserts that our moral language casts self-interest and self-sacrifice as antithetical categories, privileging self-sacrifice as the moral good. Within this conceptual framework, seeking one's own best interest is described as moral failure, as selfishness. Denying one's own interests, for the sake of another, is lauded. In inequitable power relations, however, according to ethicist Sarah Lucia Hoagland, "altruism accrues to the one in the subordinate position."[7] Furthermore, says Hoagland, "selfishness" is a label given to people who refuse to "go along with the group," and is used to "manipulate our participation toward someone else's end."[8]

Thus, the requirement of duty/obligation frequently means that out of love some must sacrifice themselves to the interests of others. This has led one critic to observe: "Family loyalty can become ultimate loyalty. Family can become the place you have to go and have to be taken in even if you don't want to be taken in, even if it means denying the self you have discovered as your real self."[9]

Gay men and lesbians frequently find that in order to be accepted by their families, they are expected to deny themselves and their most intimate relationships. Parents or siblings may tell them, "I love and accept you, but don't tell the neighbors!" This may be because parents are ashamed of their children; it could also stem from the parents' desire to protect their children from the narrow-mindedness of others. In either case, it requires the gay or lesbian family member to participate in self-denial.

This response was typical in the biological families of many of those we interviewed. In a group of lesbian couples, one woman, Ginny, recounted the following story:

> "My mother, even though she's seemingly accepting of us, she doesn't talk. Nobody else knows, like her best friends don't know, and her sister; the

> rest of the family members back on the east coast don't know. My sister Carol was having a bat mitzvah about a year ago and my mother's friend Helen was coming, and my mother, in her way, said, 'Well, you don't have to give everyone a tour of the house.' What she was really saying is, 'You don't need to tell her that you're lesbians, and don't show her your bedroom.' "

Ginny went on to say that eventually her mother agreed to tell Helen about Ginny and her partner, and that over the years her mother has become more open about her daughter's life, even though it is still difficult for her.

Not all parents and siblings are able to rise to the occasion, and many lesbians and gay men find that their families follow a "Don't ask, don't tell" policy. The men and women we spoke with told tales of covering up their gay/lesbian identity when family members came to visit. They would put away pictures of friends and partners, hide love letters, pack up books with the words "gay," "lesbian," or "homosexual" in the titles. One of the women we spoke with referred to this process as "de-lavenderizing the house." Our straight family members often don't seem to understand what they are asking of us when they require that we hide significant pieces of our lives.

In a television interview during the 1992 presidential campaign, George Bush was asked how he would respond if one of his grandchildren were to announce that she or he was homosexual. Bush began by saying he would put his arms around that grandchild, and love him. But then he went on to say that he hoped that this person would not go out and promote a homosexual lifestyle as normal; that this person would not become an advocate for homosexual marriages or homosexual rights.[10] Though Bush did not say he would stop loving the grandchild, there is a conditional aspect to this in that he hoped this person would remain apolitical.

Mutuality and Accountability

Although the men and women we interviewed revealed that the idea of unconditional love was appealing to them, their own experiences challenged them to question whether this was a value they could fully embrace or was something they wanted to create within their own chosen families. They struggled to find a language for this value that would free it from the power dynamics that had been so damaging for many of them. Kevin, one of the single men we spoke with, reflected on his own conflict about this:

> "I am wondering about some people that I thought would be my extended group of friends forever who have slipped away. For some reason that wasn't unconditional; we found that it was time to move on. Some of my friends, I still consider them extended family and lean on the kinds of support I don't get from siblings. I have an older brother that I virtually have a nonrelationship with, and my parents are supportive only to a certain extent, so I rely heavily on these other people, but I found that those relationships can be conditional as well, and that's something I'm struggling with right now."

As we listened to gay men and lesbians discuss both the joys of familial love and their own pain and disappointment when this love was withheld, we realized that the values of commitment and responsibility had to be renamed. Rather than using the concepts of duty and obligation to talk about this, we believe that the language of mutuality and accountability may allow us to retain what is best in traditional family values while avoiding the pitfalls of inequitable power relationships.

What, then, do we mean by mutuality? New research in psychology—for example, the work being done at the Stone Center for Developmental Services and Studies, at Wellesley College in Massachusetts—suggests that "mutually empathic and empowering" relationships are necessary for our well-being.[11] This insight represents a shift in traditional psychotherapeutic models of development, a shift from emphasis on individuation and separation as necessary for mental health to a model of interconnection. Those at the Stone Center caution that mutual connectedness should not be confused with dependency. This does not privilege either living for others, or living for the self, but rather wrestling with the question of how we live *with* others in ways that empower all.

Building on this insight, Episcopal priest and theologian Carter Heyward identifies mutuality as a model of friendship that provides a "basic way to experience and envision justice."[12] This model of friendship as a superior form of relationship challenges traditional notions of family. As we have discussed in chapter 2, the normative family model denigrates friendship as a less-valued form of human relationship, often summed up in the phrase "just friends." But, as theologian Mary E. Hunt points out, the biblical commandment for relationship is to love one's neighbor (not spouse or children) as oneself. Hunt defines friendship as "those voluntary human relationships that are entered into by people who intend one another's well-being and who intend that their love relationship is part of a justice-seeking community."[13]

This connection between friendship and justice is important to a discussion of mutuality and accountability. As political theorist Susan Moller Okin has argued, we will never have justice in society until we have justice in our families.[14] It is within our families that we first learn our lessons of justice and fairness, lessons we will carry with us for the rest of our lives. Although there are numerous theories of justice available, theories that attempt to explain how we can create a just society, Okin claims that these theories fall short because they ignore the injustice in the traditional family model. She points out that "most theorists *assume,* though they do not discuss, the traditional, gender-structured family."[15]

Within the traditional family model, the family division of labor is gender-based, as is the importance placed on the work men and women do, with men's roles and activity being valued more highly in society than those of women. The greater value given to male activity is carried into the family, where men are given familial authority as a "natural" right. This arrangement empowers men over and against women and their children, creating disparate relationships. The dominance and submission dualism is worked out sexually in the traditional family model. Alternatively, social ethicist Beverly Harrison argues for the value of mutuality as applied to sex:

> Sexual communication, at its best, mutually enhances self-respect and valuation of the other. The moral norm for sexual communication in a feminist ethic is radical mutuality—the simultaneous acknowledgment of vulnerability to the need of another, the recognition of one's own power to give and receive pleasure and to call forth another's power of relation and to express one's own.[16]

Mutuality is not only valid in a feminist ethic. We believe that this value is necessary to a reconstruction of family which is empowering to all participants, male and female, gay and straight, blood kin or chosen family. Moreover, valuing and respecting the other and also receiving from the other, not sacrificing ourselves for the other, should go beyond sex to strengthen our relationships generally.

Gay and Lesbian Families as Non-Gender Based

While we believe that mutuality is a positive reconstruction of relationship for all persons, we also maintain that lesbian and gay relationships, in particular, may provide a powerful model for how such mutuality may be accomplished. This is because gay and lesbian families do not, by their very nature, participate in the traditional gender-structured division of labor. Hence, they must, by necessity, create new models of relating not premised on male privilege and female subordination.

Among the women we interviewed, in particular, this sense of freedom from traditional gender roles was experienced as being very liberating. Alicia, who was once married to a man, reflected on the difference in her relationship with a woman:

> "As soon as you get married, the roles are already identified—you cook, you clean. With a lesbian couple, you don't know who is doing what! But I think as a lesbian couple you do whatever you like the most. If I cook, I cook because I like it, not because I have to cook. But in a regular marriage I have to cook all the time, so in a way we have more permission to do different things, so we are more free to find what we want to do in the household."

She went on to say that this equity extended beyond simply the household responsibilities:

> "When Sandy and I first got together there was an incredible imbalance in our salaries and our work. She was making tons of money and I was just like an average person. I think it was a struggle for me the first year or two not to feel like when we bought a house I had to pay fifty percent. When I was married, his money was my money, but there wasn't any equity. He was a man and I was just a woman and there was a lot that I had to compensate for. When I came together with a woman, it was a pressure that I wasn't going to fall into. We don't have that pressure anymore."

Since the gender-structured family is inherently unjust (privileging the husband/father over and against women and children), Susan Moller Okin argues that we learn in our families that inequitable relationships are normal and permissible.[17] Thus, we come to accept disparate power relationships as inevitable in all areas of society.

Other theorists concur with her analysis, arguing that one of the principal functions of the family (if not the principal) is to socialize us into the gender hierarchy which is the basis of U.S. culture and serves as the ideological model for all other social hierarchies.[18] Sarah Lucia Hoagland has observed that this gender hierarchy "normalizes the dominance of one person in a relationship and the subordination of another."[19] Carter Heyward further argues that this domination is romanticized in male-female relationships, and anything that deviates from male gender domination is seen as "abnormal."[20]

Mutual Empowerment and Benefit

While there will always be relationships which are characterized by inequality—parent/child, teacher/student, employer/employee—we believe that such relationships can be transformed so as to be mutually empowering and beneficial. The key to such transformation lies in a commitment to dismantling the fixed and rigid construction of inequality premised on the gender-structured inequality of the traditional family.

This does not imply commitment to a naively idealist view that we can create a radical equality within society, or even that we should desire to do so. There are times when it is necessary and appropriate that someone should exercise more authority than another. The problem, however, arises when authority is only and always granted to the same group of persons. This is the source of oppressive structures, whether racist, classist, sexist, or heterosexist.

Mutuality, as we are using the term, requires an understanding of relationship based on what Carter Heyward has called "dynamic relational movement":[21]

> In any unequal power relationship, if the structure of inequality is assumed to be static . . . the relationship cannot enable authentic empowerment. If, moreover, the effects of inequality are presumed, and even encouraged, to linger *in perpetuity* . . . the relationship will be emotionally and spiritually distorted for both, regardless of how well meaning they may be.[22]

Family theorists Kristine M. Baber and Katherine R. Allen have argued that the traditional socialization of persons within the family model makes such mutuality difficult.[23] Within this model, power accrues to the husband/father as an unquestioned right, a right which he continues to hold. As they point out, mutuality "involves reciprocal empathy and concern and requires flexibility, emotional availability, and interaction."[24]

These characteristics identified by Baber and Allen resonated with the understanding of family which the lesbians and gay men we interviewed struggled to create in their chosen families, as the following conversation demonstrates:

> "We have sort of a responsibility to, like, when emotional shit gets in the way, and things are not working, there is a level of emotional accountability that I think we have to have."
>
> "That kind of thing is on a different level, a more general ethic of care where you have a feeling to be in the other person's life in a significant way, and that would be more ongoing. I mean you can miss taking out the trash for a week and not a bad thing will happen, but if you started missing out because you weren't paying attention to the other person and just being concerned about your own things and you didn't care what was happening, then that seems like it's a different kind of thing."
>
> "I have a different model because when I was in a religious community it was a community of living together and there were people who shared values and shared goals, and I liked that model better than the traditional family model. I want to recreate that because there are people that I care about and am concerned about, and those people I'm willing to struggle with and deal with the shit, even if I don't want to."

Carter Heyward echoes this understanding in her claim that mutuality is a process that involves the struggle to share power and to work out inequality. She points out that such struggle can be painful, since the dominant institutions in our lives, premised as they are on the normativeness of inequity, resist efforts to create mutuality: "This is because, in a praxis of alienation and domination, the desire for mutuality almost invariably is punished rather than rewarded."[25] Mutuality does not require a radical equality of persons, but it does ask that we struggle with inequality; it challenges us to think about the ways in which we allocate power in our relationships and to be willing to renegotiate the balance of power.

As we stated at the outset of this discussion, we believe the lesbian/gay family structure has the potential to teach us all something about mutuality. Since these family systems operate outside the traditional gender-structured models of authority, the distribution of power, as well as duties and obligations, must be negotiated at every hand. There can be no unspoken assumption that one person will do all the caretaking work, while the other is the breadwinner. No one partner immediately is cast in the role of the primary parent, or the one who does the yard work, or the one who cleans the toilets.

Neither, however, do we want to romanticize and idealize lesbian/gay relationships. Certainly examples exist of gay men and lesbians simply recreating the traditional paradigm in the gay context rather than transcending these limiting categories and creating something new. However, we maintain that the *potential* for mutually empowering relationships is inherent in familial structures where authority and submission are not automatically allocated based on gender. It is to the potential of lesbian/gay relationships that we point.

Four of the women we interviewed shared a house, and reflected that part of the reason for their decision was to break free of the traditional model of the couple who shut themselves off from society. They wanted to attempt a more communal form of living because they saw this as a challenge to traditional, gender-structured ideas of family. For Sandy, in particular, this was a very conscious choice:

> "This is, for me, how we ended up the four of us. Because part of what I was questioning was this model—the two of us. It was just the two of us, we're not going to have kids, we've got three dogs, I have this humongous phone bill—I'm constantly trying to make connections out in the world—and I have to do something about this because it takes a toll on the relationship. It's too demanding on one other person for me to try to get all of that from her. So, for me, that was part of the thing about living communally and we ended up in this one house, but the idea of having people close by, physical access—I think that occurred as a result of questioning the model. I'm just much happier in this environment."

Mutuality as a model for familial relationship does not represent an abdication of our responsibilities to our families, whether biological or chosen. Neither, however, does it require that we sacrifice self-interest to preserve the family unity. Mutuality requires that we be accountable to both self and others and recognizes that neither love nor responsibility can be determined by formulaic prescriptions. We must be as willing to relinquish power as we are to hold it; to give love as we are to be loved.

If we reflect back on the discussion of covenant in chapter 2, we can see that mutuality fits within a covenantal model as opposed to a contract model specifying duties and obligations. The covenantal model does not deny that there will be responsibilities, and it implies that there will be benefits, but the content of these is unspecified, to be worked out over time.

Because gay men and lesbians have been denied access to the predefined roles, duties, and obligations of marriage, we have, of necessity, had to work out covenants within our committed relationships outside social norms and prescriptions for how power, authority, love, and commitment are allocated. In the best of our experiments, we offer a prophetic example of what mutual family relations might be like.

4

Giving Life

•→ Ed and John are an interracial couple. They are both professionals and have been together for a number of years. When they decided they wanted to raise a child together, they chose to pursue legal adoption. Adopting a child was not easy for them, and it took a long while to set the wheels in motion. Then Ed and John received only two days' notice before they became the parents of an interracial baby boy they named Brian.

The two men, who had never been parents before, had to prepare their home to receive this child. Friends, both gay and straight, brought over clothes, blankets, toys, and all the other things needed to care for a newborn. Both men say that their life has been totally transformed by the addition of this new life to their household. Wanting to name their child in a way that reflects both of them, they gave Brian a surname combining both their surnames.

Like most children of this recent social phenomenon that has been termed the "gayby boom," Brian is still too young for any definitive statement to be made about how well he will flourish in this home with two fathers. Ed and John want Brian to have the love and nurture of women in his life. They have plenty of women friends, aunts, cousins, and doting grandmothers to fill the bill. At this point in his young life he seems content to play and receive love from his extended family of biological relatives and Ed and John's family of friends.

Gay Men and Lesbians as Parents

Stories like this one have occurred with greater frequency in recent years. Not only are lesbians and gay men raising children from previous heterosexual marriages, they are increasingly adopting children. The availability of reproductive technologies has also provided an avenue by which same-sex couples can become parents. Rock star Melissa Etheridge and her partner, Julie Cypher, appeared on the cover of *Newsweek* with the caption: "We're Having a Baby."[1] Despite the publicity gay and lesbian parenting has received, social acceptance of the gayby boom is far from complete. Although only two states explicitly forbid adoption of children by lesbians or gay men, adoption can often be a difficult and complex process. Since same-sex partnerships are not legally recognized by the state, couples need to go through co-parent adoption to ensure custody of their child.[2] While some states are highly tolerant of adoption by same-sex couples, many others are far less tolerant. It is in parenting that gay men and lesbians provide one of the greatest challenges to the taken-for-granted order of the traditional family. At the same time, it is here and in the debate over the legality of same-sex marriage that lesbians and gay men most risk becoming invisible as they are assimilated into a heterocentric status quo.

Within a traditionalist understanding of family, the creation of new life and the nurturing of children are socially valued. Raising children has been linked in our society with heterosexual marriage with its particular role expectations for women as child rearers. Raising children in other contexts, such as within unions of heterosexual couples who are not married, by single persons, or within unions of persons of the same sex, calls into question the presuppositions of the traditional model.

We are not saying that these nontraditional configurations are ideal for raising children a priori, but neither can anyone say that the presence of a mother and father in and of itself is the ideal family form for raising children. Yet conservative social critics maintain that the decline of the traditional nuclear family is a major cause of the decline in children's well-being in American society. Barbara Defoe Whitehead's lead article in the April 1993 issue of the *Atlantic Monthly* boldly proclaims, "Dan Quayle was right." Whitehead addresses the problem of children growing up in homes disrupted by divorce. She goes on to claim, more generally, that children who do not grow up in a traditional nuclear family have fewer prospects for success in their personal relationships and will be less economically successful than children of married heterosexual parents.

Even though data may support Whitehead's claim that children do not flourish in single-parent homes disrupted by divorce, it does not follow that a two-parent home must include a man and a woman.

Furthermore, the argument Whitehead makes does not seem to take seriously the complexities of the links between gender and economics involved in raising children. Single parents charged with the primary responsibility for child rearing tend to be women who, for the most part, earn significantly less than male wage earners. Women's greater economic vulnerability translates into vulnerability for their children.

The rate of divorce in heterosexual marriage in recent decades is well documented; between 50 and 60 percent of all children born in the 1980s are expected to be children of divorce before they are eighteen.[3] Despite this trend, the resulting harm to children may well be the result not of the breakdown of the traditional family, but of family instability and economic consequences based largely on the wage gap between male and female workers. Conversely, we cannot assume that the traditional nuclear family is necessarily better than other forms of family for nurturing children.

Nevertheless, since the traditional family is the societal norm, most straight people find it difficult to conceive of childbearing and child rearing outside this configuration. Anthropologist Kath Weston reports that one of the major concerns expressed by parents of lesbians and gay men, when confronted with their children's sexuality, is that there will be no grandchildren.[4]

The men and women we interviewed acknowledged that this, indeed, was one of their parents' concerns. Tom, a gay man in his forties, acknowledged that his parents were disappointed that he did not have children:

> "They are having difficulty. My brother is straight but doesn't quite have it together to have a life partner or children, and they know I'm gay. They're fine about that—sort of—but they're not having the sort of retirement life that they had envisioned, grandchildren running around. They sort of expected family to be their leisure time in retirement, and I'm getting a heavy dose of guilt about this."

Another man in the group concurred:

> "My mother has things in the basement, and she says, 'Oh, this is for when I have grandchildren, I'm going to give them these things.' It's pretty set now, she's not going to have any."

There is an assumption that being homosexual precludes the possibility of children. Yet, when gay men and lesbians do have children, either through adoption or through reproductive technologies, it is often perceived as a perversion of the natural order.

Resistance to Gay Men and Lesbians Having Children

The stories of lesbians and gay men being denied custody of their biological children, or having custody rights severely restricted, are legion. A Virginia custody case that made national headlines serves to illustrate the point. Kay Bottoms won custody of her two-year-old grandson, Tyler, from her lesbian daughter, Sharon. Bottoms claimed that her daughter and her daughter's partner, April, were unfit role models for Tyler. The court granted custody to Kay Bottoms despite expert testimony that the child was not harmed by the family environment.

According to the court, the simple fact that Sharon was a lesbian who lived in an ongoing relationship with her partner made her unfit to raise her child. A heterosexual biological relative gained custody of Tyler against the right of the biological mother to raise her son. To many it seemed that Tyler's life would be disrupted by being forced to leave his home and mother to live with a single parent, in this case his grandmother, but apparently the court presumed that being raised by a heterosexual would be a better choice for Tyler than living with his mother, even in a loving home. The philosophy of the court reflected a traditionalist paradigm in which the life that Sharon and April shared, in and of itself, ran counter to the created, "natural" order of the family.

Sharon and April felt there was a ray of hope when a higher court overturned the previous ruling on appeal. Instead of arguing on the basis of natural law, the appeals judge stated: "The social science evidence showed that a person's sexual orientation does not strongly correlate with the person's fitness as a parent."[5] In the more pragmatic approach of the appeals judge, the well-being of the child, rather than a traditional understanding of the "natural" order of the family, became the dominant value. Conservative groups strongly protested the ruling because they claimed it violated natural law and traditional values rooted in the religious tradition of the United States. In fact, these conservative arguments carried the day in April 1995 when, upon another appeal, the previous ruling was overturned.[6]

The notion that gay men and lesbians cannot be good parents seems to persist in our society. Take, for example, a recent study in which researchers presented to college students four vignettes describing couples interested in adopting a five-year-old African American boy. The couples were described in identical terms except that they either differed ethnically (African American, white, or interracial) or were homosexual. College students who were asked to discuss the homosexual couple tended not only to state that the couple would not have a good chance at being awarded custody, but also believed that the couple's relationship would be unstable, creating a dangerous and insecure environment for the child.[7]

There are numerous examples of lesbians and gay men who not only have children, but fight for their custody, love and nurture them, and raise them to be healthy, contributing members of society. The existence of gay men and lesbians forming families with children makes available a model of family that differs from the traditional norm. Such alternative models demonstrate that families are social constructions and that children can flourish in homes with two moms, or two dads, as well as they can with heterosexual parents. While more research is needed, studies conducted to date have found that children flourish with parents of the same sex.[8]

The fact that a popular current affairs magazine such as *Newsweek* openly discussed lesbian and gay parenting in a positive light bodes well for a change in the attitudes of the majority of Americans. A recent *Newsweek* poll found that 36 percent of those surveyed think gay and lesbian couples should be able to adopt. Only 29 percent responded this way in a survey conducted in 1994. Slightly less than half of those sampled, 47 percent, opposed gay and lesbian adoption, a decrease from the 1994 survey, in which fully 65 percent of those polled opposed such adoptions.[9]

Sacrifices and Shifting Attitudes

While the rhetoric of the new right demonizes lesbians and gay parents, this emerging family form challenges the assumptions of many critics. Further, parenting has now become an option for many gay men and lesbians who previously did not think it was possible. In her book *Reinventing the Family,* Laura Berkov recalls dreaming about the possibility of parenting with her lover, but imagined that they were the only lesbians who hoped for this possibility in their lives.[10]

Berkov reflects on the word "invention" as the creation of something that did not previously exist. Inventions of this sort not only make new horizons available but also transform cultural reality. One couple we interviewed, Sandy and Barb, provide an example of lesbian parents who share Berkov's view.

Sandy and Barb have three children. Both of them were previously married to men and are now divorced. Sandy has two teenage boys and Barb has a teenage girl. They have some of the problems common to all blended families. They have had to negotiate the rules of the household. They have had to address issues of parental authority and negotiate how to discipline the children. They also have to deal with teenagers who are very conscious of their peers' responses to their mothers' relationship. At first all three children expressed a lot of resistance to the relationship. Over time, however, they have grown closer as a family and are more willing to share with friends the fact that they have two moms.

Barb and Sandy believe that the relationship they are modeling now will have profound benefits for their children in future years. Already they see their children being more open to diversity than they had been previously. Also, say the moms, the children seem to think more critically about a wide variety of issues, from politics and religion to gender roles. Barb says she feels her obligation as a mother is to make the next generation more genuinely human than the one before it. She believes she is meeting that goal by modeling a loving relationship with another person even if the gender of the other person does not fit social expectations. Her relationship with Sandy, she believes, will help her children see people, not a label, first.[11]

Becoming parents often brings tremendous costs, whether the parents are gay or straight. It may be extremely difficult and expensive, especially if parents are adopting or find it necessary to use various forms of reproductive technology. In addition, parenthood brings changes in personal relationships; it even brings a transformation in personal identity and changes the ways others view our identities. Parenting also requires a tremendous investment of expense, time, and effort. What makes the sacrifices of gay men and lesbians distinct?

Whereas for heterosexual couples the norms of the broader society fully support giving birth and raising children, same-sex couples, and even heterosexual single parents, find that in addition to the normal demands of parenting they must also fight against societal norms. Phyllis Burke, in her moving book *Family Values: A Lesbian Mother's Fight for Her Son,* recounts her struggle to adopt Jesse, her partner Cheryl's biological son. This book reveals many of the ways in which social norms work against lesbian and gay parents. Phyllis and Cheryl's long fight with city officials in San Francisco represents both a struggle for the legal recognition of their family and a tribute to the commitment these two women have to their child.[12]

In addition to lacking support from straight society, gay parents do not always find total support in the gay and lesbian community. Attitudes about parenting within the gay community are divided, and there are those who will oppose or not support those who decide to parent. For some gay men and lesbians, the possibility of having children challenges their image of what it means to be gay or lesbian.

Ed and John, whose story began this chapter, participated in one of our focus groups. They noted that gay friends did not always respond positively to the news of their adoption. "They [have] set up their lives with the intention of not having children," Ed said. For these friends, the fact that gay men whom they knew were having a child challenged the way they viewed the world. "This was something they never thought they could do."

Some of John and Ed's friends were critical of the adoption; others eventually dropped out of their social network. Ed commented that adopting a child caused him to reevaluate who the members of his "gay family" really were:

> "You know, family are people who really stay with you. We have had people we considered family and they haven't stayed with us—but parts of our gay family have."

John, his partner, added:

> "One of the things we noticed was that most of our friends treated us differently when Brian was born. They either got closer or more distant."

Both men agreed that the friends with whom they had once been close had a different relationship with them after Brian's birth.

Experiences like Ed and John's are not the only reality, however. Charlene, who was pregnant with twins when she and her partner, Sally, attended a focus group, mentioned how much support she has felt from all her chosen family, both gay and straight. Charlene and Sally had been thinking about having a child for nearly ten years. They decided they wanted to have a child who was biologically related to one of them, and that Charlene would be the birth mother utilizing artificial insemination. The sperm donor is a friend of theirs and is still part of their close family of friends. The women discussed the fact that their chosen family have been cheering them on. Sally added:

> "Our family of friends are going to be very involved. We want to call them aunts or guardian angels or whatever so that they have a relationship with the children from the very first."

The Politics of Parenthood

Whether or not one's chosen family is able to integrate new parents and a child into the family circle, parenting does demand a reexamining of identity by previously childless people. For lesbian and gay parents, redefining identity in light of being a parent raises questions concerning the political implications of parenthood. Does parenthood redefine our identity so that we simply become part of the norm without challenging it?

Comments from men and women in our focus group helped us to reflect on this question. Sally told us:

> "When we were growing up, family was really centered around children. So now I think we've really come full circle having a baby."

Another lesbian couple, Marie and Nina, are attempting to have a child through artificial insemination. Marie recalled a conversation she had with a woman she had just met:

> "I had a situation where I was in a conversation with a person and they asked if I was married and I said 'yes.' They asked if I had children and I said, 'We're considering it.' I left the conversation realizing that I had just passed for being heterosexual. It seemed like a lot of trouble to go through a big explanation that I'm a lesbian and I'm married to a wonderful woman and we want to have children. I'm having to deal with things in a way I

> haven't had to before. I don't want to pass as heterosexual, but I don't want to necessarily have that discussion with everyone."

Marie felt a conflict between the need to tell about her experience as a lesbian in a committed relationship with another woman with whom she wanted to raise a child and her desire to keep her life private.

Marie's story reveals the ways in which issues generally understood as "private" family matters can become political issues. Had Marie been a straight woman having difficulty getting pregnant, she would not have even considered explaining that she was married to a wonderful man with a low sperm count, for example.

Gay men and lesbians who have children face the dilemma of coming out as gay or lesbian parents in social settings, or simply passing as a straight parent. Sally commented that since Charlene's pregnancy, strangers have approached them and asked to touch her belly. When faced with that situation, she believes one has to decide whether to turn it into an opportunity to come out. Charlene added that her pregnancy has provided her with many opportunities to tell people she is both a lesbian and a mother-to-be:

> "Coming out is a big deal for me because I teach high school. It's been wonderful because it brings up these great situations where a student will come up and say: 'Hey, who's the lucky guy?' and I say, 'Woman?' They say, 'What?' 'Well, you're referring to my mate aren't you?' And they say, 'Yeah.' 'Well, my mate's a woman.' They say, 'Wait a minute; I thought I knew how people got pregnant.' It's just sort of light like that, and that's been fun. I've found that when you are pregnant, when you have babies, there is a kind of normalcy, you are okay in a way. People accept you. It's been a positive way of coming out. In a way, when you are a lesbian, you are rejecting tradition. Having children, you're accepting your role as a woman somewhat."

Charlene's perspective touches on one way in which having a child demonstrates that lesbians and gay men have multifaceted identities. Yet her comment suggests a potential problem. Does having children make lesbians, in particular, less of a threat to the status quo? Does having children demonstrate that lesbians can "accept their role as childbearers"? Is the cultural code of the "standard American family" finding its expression in lesbians and gay men who want to settle down and have children? [13] Lesbians and gay men who decide to have children are making that choice outside the bounds of traditional marriage. By that very action, they make a statement that challenges the patriarchal notions of the nuclear family.

It seems to us that the chief contribution lesbian and gay parents can make toward changing narrow societal views is to come out as gay and lesbian parents. As Ed commented, when he and John take their son Brian to the park and talk with other parents, the fact that they are gay recedes in importance. Straight people can relate as parents. In this sense, the act of partnering and parenting is a creative act in that it opens the horizons and transforms the categories that our society gives us.

Feminist scholar Anna Jonasdottir discusses the political nature of the gender-sexual relations between men and women and the reproduction of human beings in modern Western societies. She argues that social differences between women and men are rooted in the ways patriarchal societies construct love and sexuality. There is a gendered division of love in which "women, to a greater *degree* than men, and in different ways, initiate, pursue, and support issues concerning biosocial production, that is, those questions having to do with control over, responsibility for, and care of people, and other natural resources."[14] In the traditionalist model of the family, women provide intimate caring to a greater extent than men do. They also are responsible for bearing and raising children and in maintaining the ties between extended family members to a larger degree than men are.

Several of the lesbian women we interviewed discussed the ways they had internalized these gender role expectations:

> "Women's programming, our socialization, teaches us that we are the ones who are responsible for keeping the relationship together. The men know that somebody else is there to keep the home fires burning and they can go out and sow their seed."

Another woman agreed:

> "That's part of our job as girls, when we grow up. We're responsible for the relationship. We are responsible to make sure that everybody is happy and that everybody gets a chance to participate, and all of the B.S. that goes along with being female."

These women went on to say that part of what they found liberating in lesbian relationships was that they were freed from these gender expectations. Thus lesbians, and especially gay men, who have children are a challenge to the social division of love.

The Power of Creativity and Generativity

In addition to procreation, our focus in the earlier section of this chapter, there are other dimensions of what is meant by the term "giving life." One such dimension is to be creative. The power of creation is the power to bring something new into being. Creativity, as Elizabeth Say has argued elsewhere, is not a rejection of what has gone on before in order to bring about something entirely new. "It is the ability to bring a new vision of existent conceptions, and to do so in a way that they become authentic for others."[15] In creativity, we transcend the limits imposed by received definitions of reality; we create new vision.

This new vision of giving life is a creativity born of the potentially transformative role of gay and lesbian parents, and in the potential for social transformation within the loving unions of gay men and lesbians. In addition, we give life to each other through the creative ways in which we transform ourselves through our relationships with our partners and our chosen families. We do not remain the persons we were when we entered relationships with our partners or our families of choice. Through these relationships we come to a greater awareness of who we are becoming.

In setting out this understanding of creativity and vision, we make space for gay men and lesbians who do not choose to have children. We maintain that such men and women are still generative, still can give life, by providing a place where members of our chosen families can express themselves. Moreover, our chosen families are places in which those who may not fit the received norms can find a haven. Homes of lesbians and gay men can give life through hospitality shown to others. Particularly at holiday times, the hospitality of gay and lesbian friends can provide an atmosphere of celebration especially when relations with biological kin are strained or broken. We believe that the creation of lesbian and gay family homes can serve as a prophetic reminder to ourselves to open our doors and ourselves in hospitality to the "other," the stranger in our midst. Giving life through hospitality brings to mind the ancient biblical injunction to be hospitable, since all lesbians and gay men have themselves been strangers and aliens to one extent or another.

Kevin and Nathan, two gay brothers who participated in a focus group, discussed their understanding of hospitality as a family value:

> "We grew up in a household where people were coming in all of the time, dropping by. The rule on holidays was to fill the table; no one should ever be alone, so you bring everybody in. Friends from work, all types of people that my parents were doing business with. There were always people over at the house. We spent seven to eight hours at the table on holidays and people came in, and the dishes changed, so our exposure to a wide variety of people was amazing."

Another member of this group commented:

> "To me that teaches you acceptance of anybody and who they are; to me that's a really good family value to learn."

Creating new life, then, can be understood in terms of the new life we create with our chosen families.

Broader models of what it means to give life have been explored in other contexts. For example, Betty Friedan has used the concept of generativity to refer to the creative expressions of older Americans. Friedan recounts stories of people who, as they grow older, seek to move beyond caring for their biological families and attempt to give life to their communities. "How do we find ways," she writes, "as we feel we must, to use the wisdom we have derived from the painful, joyful experiences of our lives as we have lived them, *in society,* so that we may live out our generativity?"[16] Friedan reminds us that old age is not necessarily a time when productivity is diminished. Rather, old age can be a time in which generativity becomes redefined to include nurturing our communities with our wisdom and care.

Friedan's perspective illuminates the opportunities of gay men and lesbians to live out their generativity, to give life to others. Often, through the loneliness and isolation they experienced from the broader society, they were available to give themselves fully to service of others. In his book *Virtually Normal: An Argument about Homosexuality,* Andrew Sullivan has written about this social role of homosexual people:

> Childless men and women have many things to offer a society. They can transfer their parental instincts into broader parental roles: they can be extraordinary teachers and mentors, nurses and doctors, priests, rabbis and nuns; they can throw themselves into charity work, helping the needy and the lonely; they can care for the young who have been abandoned by others, through adoption. Or they can use all their spare time to forge an excellence in their field of work that is sometimes unavailable to the harried mother or the burdened father.[17]

Sullivan's insight was brought home to us through a story told by Kevin, one of the gay brothers discussed earlier, who is also a middle-school teacher.

> "Most of my kids [students] are in the riot zone, downtown L.A., broken families. Someone will call me daddy; they hug you, they cry with you, and they don't let everybody know they do that with you because that's not cool. Some of them see me more than they see anyone else in their own family. I have a little boy who just latches on to me. He's there at 7:30 in the morning to help carry my bags for me. I drive him home and he's just overwhelmed that somebody's worried about him. I took thirty kids camping for three days. We went in this pool, swimming, and they just could not stay away because I was spending time with them. They're ten to eleven years old; this one little boy hopped up and hugged me and threw his arms around me like he was a five-year-old, and just would not let go, because it was someone who cared about him, unconditionally."

Kevin's experience illustrates the ways in which gay men and lesbians can help children flourish without being parents and also demonstrates a way in which we can be generative to a broader community.

A much-neglected avenue for sharing our generativity exists in the rich possibilities of intergenerational sharing between members of gay and lesbian communities. A question we might ask is how our chosen families can become more inclusive of different generations of gay men and lesbians. Our families of choice can become exclusionary to those who are not like us. Sharing across the generations is a source of wisdom and insight for young and old alike.

One of our focus groups had an interesting conversation about this need for gay and lesbian communities to be more responsive to generations that have come before and those that will follow. One of the gay men in this group, Kevin, expressed his opinion:

> "One thing the family means to me is a concern for the next generation. I think about what my responsibility to teenagers is—I mean, they get talked about in certain political circles in the gay community, but it's not a general orientation to care about this younger generation, or the older generation. A lot of people have run away from those kinds of responsibilities, but as a community that is maturing now, we need to start thinking about the coming generation and what sort of responsibilities we have. That's a family value!"

Finally, nurturing and generativity are values that have been developed in the lesbian and gay communities, ironically, in the age of AIDS. In the midst of death and disease, new lessons have been learned of giving beyond ourselves to others in need. Caring for the sick has not only strengthened the bonds of our chosen families, but has also been the catalyst by which many gay men in particular have come to a renewed sense of activism and community involvement. This lesson has been a costly one. We can only hope that a desire to create families either in extended kin networks, or through raising children, will not lessen our public involvement in nurturing our communities.

Identity and Community

Cathy tells her story as we sit having lunch in a coffee shop in Orange County, California. Cathy wears blue slacks and a crisp white blouse. Her curly salt-and-pepper hair is pulled back enough to reveal rainbow-colored gay pride earrings. She sips a cup of herbal tea while we talk. Cathy has a master's degree in social work. She has led a quiet and fairly sheltered life.

She knew her husband in high school. After marriage, they adopted two multiracial children and were married for twenty years. After only a few years of marriage, however, Cathy began to become aware that she was a lesbian. She remained in her marriage to give the children a stable home environment, but was increasingly dissatisfied with this arrangement. It seemed to her that a whole aspect of her identity was being submerged.

In time she met Linda at work and they became friends. When Cathy and Linda became romantically involved, Cathy felt the need to leave her marriage. Cathy has struggled to keep her own sense of self while trying to embrace her lesbian identity. She complains that some lesbians are suspicious of her because she was married for so many years and is a mother. She believes that some women in the gay community have a narrow understanding of what it means to be a lesbian. "I don't have to wear my hair in a certain way or wear a leather jacket; I'm just me. I don't have to look or act in a certain way."

Cathy has integrated her sexual identity with the rest of her life as a social worker and therapist, as a mother, and as a member of her church. She still attends the church she and her husband both attended for many years. She talks about the difficulty of trying to keep together all the different aspects of who she is. People who knew her before she came out have also had trouble coming to understand Cathy as a lesbian, a mother, and the friend they have known for years. The difficulty of understanding who she is was perhaps best expressed by her son's teenage friend: "She can't be a lesbian, she's Carter's mom."

Families as Sources of Identity

Cathy's story describes yet another family value—that of identity. The men and women we interviewed spoke of both their biological families and their chosen families as a source of their identity and as a site of community with others like themselves. At the same time, these men and women acknowledged that their identity as gay men or lesbians often divided them from their families of origin and that they frequently felt torn between competing identities and communities.

As we have discussed, our society privileges the biological family unit over other social groupings that affect the creation of self-identity. The biological family is understood as a primary source of our identity. For the majority of Americans, the family helps us to know where we came from. It provides a history in which we can find ourselves; it gives us a sense of belonging and heritage.

Embedded in familial relations are other aspects of identity and belonging, such as ethnic or religious ties. Part of the requirement of familial loyalty is that we are to honor the traditions of our parents and their parents before them. So, for example, we identify ourselves as Irish Catholic, Southern Baptist, Eastern European Jew, or whatever. We are linked not only to a particular biological network but to a cultural identity as well. This may take the form of celebrating certain holidays, appreciating particular foods or music, or preserving a language within the family. Such practices give richness and texture to our lives and further inform our sense of our selves.

Alicia, a Cuban American woman who participated in one of our focus groups, told us that she grew up with a strong sense of family linked to ethnic identity. Her family attempted to preserve their cultural heritage when they came to the United States. Other Cuban Americans, who were not related by blood, became as close as biological family because of the ethnic ties they shared in a foreign culture.

> "These family friends were part of the group and shared with us those Cuban values and customs. It was part of our family values to hang on to

our culture and those traditions of the old country, to preserve that and bring up the kids and keep them with their language."

Ethnic or religious identification may also place limits or restrictions on self-discovery. To choose a marriage partner outside the community, for example, has frequently been seen as a betrayal of one's family or ethnic group. Certainly marrying outside one's ethnic group can serve to dilute that cultural presence in American society. Among American Jews, for example, intermarriage is a growing trend that some argue is eroding Jewish culture in American society. A few years ago, as part of a lecture series at Tulane University on American religion, the late Rabbi Marc Tannenbaum commented wryly on the feelings of many American Jews regarding intermarriage: "Should we have survived the Holocaust only to be destroyed by love?" Even though our ethnic communities, and our culture as a whole, value knowing our heritage as a source of our identity, the quest for identity occurs within a complex web of relationships, not all of which are determined by biological kinship.

The Need to Separate

As many lesbians and gay men know, coming to terms with one's own sexual identity frequently means risking separation from one's biological family or at least not being acknowledged as who one really is. In fact, many gay men and lesbians recount that they felt like outsiders within their own families from a young age, never really enjoying the promised sense of belonging.

In his autobiographical novel *A Boy's Own Story,* Edmund White poignantly captures this experience. Here he reflects on his memory of an evening out with his family: *"I don't belong here,* I shouted at them silently. . . . I wanted the white and gold doors to open as my loving, true but not-yet-found friends came toward me, their gently smiling faces lit from below by candles on the cake. This longing for lovers and friends was so full within me that it could spill over at any provocation."[1] White's childhood fantasy depicts not only a sense of isolation, but a longing for a community of friends through whom he might find his own identity.

One of the women who participated in our focus groups remembered a similar longing before she came out:

> "I felt always that I had to go outside of my family. It's not that I have been cut off from my family; they're kind people. They are never judging of me because I'm a lesbian. They're nice, liberal, open-minded people, but there was some lack of connectedness and something in the way they interacted. I felt dissatisfied with the substance of it."

Many of the men and women we interviewed said that the biological family was not the place where they gained a sense of who they were. Many complained that they were known only superficially in their biological families. The following conversation emerged in a group of single gay men:

> "My feeling, that I think a lot of people have, is that if they were really paying attention, if they really loved me, if they really cared about me, they would have figured it out. When I would be evasive and I wouldn't quite answer this question, they would care enough to take that extra step. Maybe that's just a childhood fantasy."
>
> "I think the compelling theme of family values is that we want them to recognize and understand us without us having to go through it all [the coming-out process]. Because if they really knew us they would know."
>
> "This whole notion of parents figuring it out is ubiquitous. It goes way back; we're not verbal until we're two or three and our parents figure out what our needs are. We don't have to tell them, yet somehow they figure out what we need. So I think there is a strong need with all of us to have our parents figure out what's going on."

These men had hoped their families would know them for who they really were, and provide a safe place where they could both articulate their identity as gay men and integrate the life of a gay man into the life of the family. They carried the need to be known for who one is into other relationships as well.

Often, for gay men and lesbians, the fear that those we love will reject us causes us to remain secretive for a long period of time. For some, however, revealing one's identity is necessary in order to have a meaningful relationship with their family members. This sentiment was expressed in a group of single men and women:

> "It was important for me to come out to my mother and father because there was no communication. It was this superficial crap, and I just finally got real tired of it. You do get tired of hiding yourself. I just wanted this

out; it would make things easier or worse. They were worse for a while, but they got better."

"I came out because I was tired of not sharing my life with my family and I felt like we were talking about garbage; there was no substance. And how am I going to get close to you unless I see this as part of my responsibility as a member of the family and contributing. I sort of said, 'Look, this is me. You accept me or not. You talk to me or not, but I'm not going to take any more responsibility for not talking about me.'"

These comments reveal that not only do we want the family to be a place where we gain a sense of who we are, but also the place where we can be known and loved for who we are.

Naming Our Relationships

Even when gay men and lesbians are accepted into the family, biological family members may still find it difficult to integrate the life of their son, daughter, brother, or sister into the life of the family. As one lesbian woman explained to us:

> "For the most part, I think my family is fine with my relationship—but they don't talk, they don't say the lesbian word or the gay word."

Thus, even though her family seemingly accepts her as a lesbian, there is a barrier of silence that continues to deny her identity. Another woman in the group had a similar experience to share:

> "The family had some big event—some anniversary—and I wanted to include Natalie, and I had a confrontation with my mother. I didn't feel comfortable going if Natalie couldn't go, but I didn't want to bring Natalie if the people there didn't know who Natalie was to me. I actually confronted my mother and said these things. My brother-in-law was always included in these events because he was family, and Natalie wasn't."

This woman felt that the significance of her relationship, a relationship of many years' duration, was not acknowledged by the biological family. Her partner did not receive the same acknowledgment that a wife or husband of a family member receives.

Bill, a man nearing retirement, commented that it seems straight people are uncomfortable hearing a gay couple talk in terms of "we" and "us." So, as gay men and lesbians, we find ourselves saying instead, "a friend and I." This insight is perhaps all the more poignant in that Bill has been in a relationship with his partner, Clint, for over thirty years.

Our biological family members seem unaware of the linguistic juggling they often expect of gay and lesbian family members. A lesbian or gay couple is "we" when at home and with their chosen family, but when we are with biological family members the subject of our sentences becomes "I," responding to a subtle pressure to disclaim the "we-ness" of our lives. Thus, for gay men and lesbians, our identity is often formed outside the biological family unit, and in tension with it. Instead of being the place where we are "really known," it is often the place where we are only partially known, and where we are required to participate in the denial of our selves.

Further, comments from the focus groups and interviews convey the problems of accepting different models in the traditional family. Since the broader society has no word for a committed relationship other than heterosexual marriage, gay and lesbian relationships are often named as something less than what they are. Calling a son's or daughter's life partner a "friend" or a "roommate" is to diminish the significance of the relationship. While biological families may believe they are accepting a gay or lesbian family member, they do not integrate their lives into the family if they fail to recognize their child or sibling as someone who is also in a long-term relationship, akin to marriage.

Becoming a married person has traditionally been a mark of taking responsibility and becoming an adult in our society, but gay men and lesbians have no socially recognized rituals or states of life that are equivalent to heterosexual marriage. As a result, families tend not only to view gay and lesbian partnerships as second rate, but to consider these family members not quite "grown up."

It is no surprise, then, that coming out to one's family is often a difficult time for gay men and lesbians. Of course, there are many cases in which biological families have fully accepted and integrated a gay man or lesbian into the family. In fact, family members themselves have often come out in a way through their public support of a lesbian or gay child or sibling. Perhaps the best example of this is Parents and Friends of Lesbians and Gays (PFLAG), a national organization for families of gay men and lesbians. PFLAG has sought to bring about more widespread social acceptance of lesbians and gay men.[2]

Pulling the Selves Together

Accepting and integrating a gay or lesbian identity, and integrating that identity within the family, raises another set of questions: What is the nature of a gay or lesbian identity? Is it formed within the gay or lesbian community (as though it were monolithic)? Don't lesbians and gay men find meaning and identity in many different communities?

Cathy's story, told at the start of this chapter, illustrates some of these issues. Cathy experienced frustration in integrating who she had been with her more recent understanding of herself as a lesbian. She understood herself to have many identities, not only as a lesbian, but as a professional woman, a mother, and a Christian. This understanding of self as plural and multifaceted provides a more complete picture of ourselves than does a flattened identity as being only a gay or lesbian person. Nevertheless, our sexual identities tend to be our most salient characteristic in public discourse, which fails to see us as complex persons encompassing multiple identities embedded in a web of relationships.

Thirty years ago, sociologists Peter Berger and Thomas Luckman observed that identity exists in a dialectical relationship with society. "Identity is formed by social processes," they write. "Once crystallized, it is maintained, modified, or even reshaped by social relations."[3] Our ideas concerning what it means to be a self are in a dynamic process, being shaped within the context of our social relations. Yet, in any given society, there are certain identities that are taken for granted and that ignore the process of identity formation that Berger and Luckman point to: being a spouse and a parent, for example, or a sibling, or a friend. These identities carry with them implied assumptions about social and sexual relations.

Alternative relationships or identities that call into question the underlying assumptions of heterosexuality, family, and friendship are understood as socially deviant. These aspects of ourselves that challenge the established order become the primary identity that the broader society sees. We are gay men or lesbians, and other aspects of who we are become subsumed under that dominant identity.

Some of the lesbians we interviewed joked about what they called the "lesbian mythology":

> "There is a mythology that you always want the same thing because you are so totally like the other person."
>
> "And that you are always about the same size!"
>
> "And that it will be good for a while and then you aren't attracted anymore, but that's okay, that's how it is with lesbians—you hug a lot!"

Though these women laughed at these ideas, they believed that the stereotype operated, in the minds of many, to deny them anything but a shallow and trivialized identity.

We live in a web of relationships with others that give us much fuller identities as partners, as family, as friends. Who we are cannot be equated simply with our sexual identity. While part of who we are as gay men or lesbians is that we have sex with people of the same gender, aren't our identities much more complex?

Writer Bruce Bawer is correct, at least on this point, when he discusses the identification of gay people with sex. He has been criticized for being "sex-negative" by some members of the gay community. Rather, Bawer explains, he has questioned the acceptance of the label that identifies us as primarily sexual beings. While our sexual orientation may be what makes us gay, "our sexual orientation doesn't define us any more than straights are defined by their orientation."[4]

The Role of Sex and Sexual Community

Even though Bawer emphasizes the complexities of gay identity, and downplays sex as the defining characteristic of that identity, a strong movement exists within the gay community to form an identity based on having sex. Bill, an older gay man who has been part of the gay liberation movement since before Stonewall, discussed the importance of sex for the gay community, especially before the onslaught of AIDS. It was having sex that linked one to the broader gay community. In the early 1970s, Bill recalled that going to the baths to have sex with many partners gave gay men "a sense of universal marriage with the whole gay community." Still, sex was not the only thing that mattered. Bill discussed the ways that being involved with a larger political and social struggle for equality also helped to form an identity as a gay person.

Even today, Bill and his partner, Clint, are involved with a variety of gay and lesbian political and social groups. Clint commented that his identity as a gay man is supported through these relationships with the gay community and with the gay family of friends. Maintaining relationships with other gay and lesbian people, Clint reflected, is necessary "in an alien and hostile society":

> "Gay people need support—the straight society has built-in support for who you are, giving you recognition. Being part of the gay community is very important to us, versus being part of an isolated couple in a nonsupportive world."

Clint and Bill's desire to be part of a larger community of gay and lesbian people was echoed by several of those we interviewed. In addition, our gay and lesbian communities and identities often incorporate other aspects of our identities, (e.g., ethnic identity, religious affiliation, cultural background). All too often, however, *the* gay or *the* lesbian community has been defined by middle-class white men or women (more in chapter 9). While these are communities that have developed a culture, there are other communities of gay and lesbian people who are excluded when one form of gay or lesbian community is held up as the norm. As one of the gay men we interviewed explained it:

> "In a broader context, gay and lesbian people are living in different cultures. I think we tend to focus on the strip in West Hollywood as what it's all about, but it doesn't have to be that way."

While identity as a gay man or lesbian is formed and sustained in the midst of relationships and in the midst of a broader gay and lesbian community, that community may be perceived as having too narrow a definition of what it means to be a gay man or lesbian. Cathy's story revealed her belief that it was difficult for some of the women she knew to understand her as a mother who had also been married to a man, as well as a lesbian. She was frustrated by the view of some lesbians that you have to dress a certain way and wear your hair a certain way to be truly a lesbian.

Narrow definitions concerning a gay or lesbian identity remove the common aspect of our identities from the center of discourse—our desire to love someone of our own sex and to have our relationships valued and respected in the same way that heterosexual relationships are valued and respected. This aspect of our identities is the source of our oppression;

this aspect of our identities calls into question the so-called naturalness of straight definitions of families.

Placing other aspects of lesbian or gay identity (such as styles of dress or political affiliations) at the center of the definition of who is lesbian or gay and who is not, or saying that identity as a gay man or lesbian carries with it a certain way of acting, a certain code, renders invisible those individuals who do not conform to these norms. Perhaps, more to the point, such things blunt the political edge of gay and lesbian identity by continuing to offer a flattened identity to the public eye.

In her essay on lesbian identity, writer Norah Vincent argues that "being an *I* first frustrates persecution by threading lesbianism so completely through the fabric of 'the norm' that it cannot be separated from it."[5] A ghettoized understanding of lesbian or gay identity does not ultimately challenge the dominant society. Living within the view of the dominant society, sharing other aspects of our identities with straight people in society, as co-workers, friends, mothers, fathers, spouses, *and* gay or lesbian people, confronts the stereotypical constructions in our society of what it means to be a lesbian or gay person and what it means to be family.

Nevertheless, there is a risk in this more assimilationist argument. Living a lifestyle woven into the fabric of "the heterosexual norm" may well lead to the continued invisibility of lesbians and gay men within the broader society. Will the families and communities of friends that help to shape who we are and give us personal satisfaction leave the dominant norms unchallenged?

Despite the conflicts that exist in attempts to identify a broader understanding of "gay and lesbian culture," the men and women we interviewed continued to affirm the importance of the more immediate community of lesbian and gay friendships in their own lives. These friends formed the extended family for many men and women, especially important for those who no longer felt "at home" with their biological families. In one of our focus groups, Allan, a single man, reported:

> "We have what we call 'orphan' get-togethers [for holidays]. You get together with friends, so you have that extended relationship. There's a desire to create a celebration of life."

Kevin, also a single man, responded with his experience of sharing a holiday away from his biological family:

> "I was living in Chicago and my parents were elsewhere, and I thought life is too short a span of time, so I stayed for Thanksgiving. I was really nervous about telling my parents, 'I'm not going to come home for Thanksgiving this year.' I went to a potluck dinner with about thirty people, mostly gay and lesbian, lots of great food and wine."

Hannah, a single woman in her forties, commented:

> "There are some women in the community that I am fairly close to. That's where I do Thanksgiving. In the lesbian community there is a lot of willingness to hang out with people that you're not lovers with, or not intending to be lovers with because we have something to talk about, we have good conversation, and that's kind of familial."

Although Allan, Kevin, and Hannah did not have partners, they all expressed a desire to share their lives with a gay family of friends. These chosen families serve as networks of love and support in the midst of a larger society in which our experiences as lesbians or gay men are often perceived as "other" or foreign.

The challenge for gay and lesbian communities is to allow our chosen families to be places where we gain personal fulfillment and come to understand who we are as gay and lesbian people, on the one hand. On the other, we must continue to confront the stereotypical conceptions of who we are and what it means to be family. That sort of challenge does not go on only in court battles, in demonstrations, or in newspaper editorials. The work of challenging the traditional understanding of what a family is, and who we are as gay or lesbian people, as parents, as siblings, as partners, and as friends also takes place in the day-to-day encounters in which the "normal" and the "natural," the taken-for-granted, is unmasked as only one way of being and living. The real challenge occurs when someone realizes, through experience, that their assumptions "ain't necessarily so," and changes their outlook in response. The process of social and political change perhaps continues most profoundly in the moments in which one person, like Cathy's son's teenage friend, confronts a reality that shakes his worldview and puzzles: "She can't be a lesbian, she's Carter's mom."

6

Erotic Power

•→ I want words for my uniquely queer experience, an as yet unheard lexicon that embodies my queer life as surely as Yiddish and Ladino did for my old Jewish grandmothers.

I want a word for who my Cuban girlfriend is to me that isn't girlfriend, partner, lover, or roommate and that encompasses how we come together hard sometimes like two fiery worlds colliding and so easy sometimes like slipping into the Caribbean sea on a steamy day.

I want a word for queer family that's about *meschpuchah,* which roughly translated from Yiddish means "The whole f—ing extended family," and that's also about invention and vision.

I want a word that says we queers are the unifiers because we live and love in every culture, race, religion, class, age, sex, tribe, village, town, city, country in the world, and we do it passionately across every single one of these constructed human boundaries.

I want a word for the kind of a world we're trying to make where fun, hot, sexy, and profoundly moral all mean the same thing.

Because I can't envision a new way of being without the words to describe it.

—Sandra Golvin, "Chinese Medicine"

The Focus on Genital Sex

We turn now to one final value we wish to explore, namely, erotic power. It may seem strange to some that we name erotic power among our family values; to some it may even seem inappropriate. Yet we believe that the erotic, properly understood, is central to familial well-being and, in particular, is critical to the self-understanding of lesbians and gay men.

The religious and conservative right do not have much to say about the erotic, although they have plenty to say about sex and sexuality, much of it negative. Many conservatives point to unbridled sexuality as the cause of contemporary social problems such as teen pregnancy, skyrocketing divorce rates, and the spread of AIDS and other sexually transmitted diseases. When sexuality does enter into discussions of traditional family values, it is usually to point to ways to protect children from sex before marriage and to reaffirm the value of sexual monogamy between spouses.

The erotic is absent from discussions of traditional family values because popular culture has reduced it to genital sexuality. Although genital sexuality is at the center of the heterosexual family, this centering often makes it appear to be beyond critique or discussion. Because it is assumed that within heterosexual marriage, sexual intercourse is not only natural but also necessary (for the purpose of procreation), there is little need to discuss it except when problems arise.

Because we accept that husbands and wives will have a sexual relationship, and because this is thought to be natural (beyond the scope of sociopolitical analysis), only when the sexual relationship breaks down do experts find it necessary to intervene. Thus, there are a host of self-help materials geared toward keeping sexual interest alive within marriage. In more recent years, these experts have extended their concerns to preventing sexual problems in the first place; marriage counseling and other forms of intervention work on sexual communication as a necessary component for a happy marriage. In the past few decades attention has also been paid to the ways in which sexual relations, even within traditional marriages, can as easily be violent and abusive as they can be expressions of love. But rarely is sexuality itself raised as an issue for discussion; sexuality and marriage go hand in hand.

In contrast, sexuality seems to be the focus of heterosexual discussions about lesbian/gay relationships: the assumption is that, in contrast with what happens in heterosexual relationships, all that lesbians and gay men do is have sex. As we discussed in chapter 5, lesbian and gay sexuality is perceived to be the defining characteristic of lesbian and gay identity. Lesbian and gay relationships are reduced to the merely sexual, and sexuality is reduced to only genital sexual activity.

Further, because homosexual sexual activity is defined as unnatural, this sexual activity becomes the focus for the analysis of the morality of the relationship. It is clear that at the heart of conservative attacks on homosexuality is an extreme reaction against gay and lesbian sex acts in and of themselves. It does not matter that we are good citizens, good neighbors, hard workers, caring and compassionate friends, even faithful members of religious congregations. Because of our sexual lives we are viewed as evil, and denounced as if we were murderers, rapists, and thieves.

One of the lesbians we interviewed acknowledged that her brother's attitude toward her reflected this point of view:

> "My brother, he's nice to me, and now that my mother has died, he calls. I don't know if he knows I am a lesbian, but he suspects something. He always wants to send somebody from the church to the house—he just doesn't picture me as gay. 'Do you have any sex problems?' he asks me. I say, 'I have a lot of problems, but not sex problems.'"

Another lesbian, Hannah, expressed the opinion that many in heterosexual society blame gays and lesbians for what is perceived as a too-permissive attitude toward sex in contemporary society:

> "I think a big part of the underlying issue of what is viewed as the problem with families is that we have a huge society full of people that are focused on sex and focused on immediate pleasure; that started a long time ago, and we opened the gate, the floodwaters, and now we are trying to redirect it because we think that's the cause of all these other problems. AIDS is one of those more visible problems, but it's easy to attach all of these other problems to extroverted sexual activities. The same people who are preaching this, who are primarily anti-gay, are also anti-abortion. The whole reason for that is, you know, keep your legs together, it's not about an abortion, it's about not having sex with whom you choose, when you choose. I think that in the gay community there's a whole different meaning."

In the face of the attitudes of society, reflected in our focus group discussions, we find it necessary to do two things in response: first, we must reclaim sexuality as a positive expression of our commitments; and second, we must expand our understanding of the erotic beyond simple genital sexuality.

Sexuality as Expressive of Commitments

The consideration of sexuality as an important dimension of human existence cannot be separated from our earlier discussion of identity formation. If identity is a social construction, then we must consider all aspects of identity as part of this process, including sexuality. Eleanor H. Haney has argued that the social construction of sexuality in Western Christian ethics can be traced back to St. Augustine, and is characterized by three primary assumptions.[1] First is the relationship of body and soul. The right relationship of the body to the soul is obedience, but because of sin the body disobeys, resulting in a loss of control over sexual impulses. Second is the emphasis on procreation, the only appropriate purpose for sexual intercourse. Third is that Western attitudes toward sexuality are characterized by sexism, misogyny, and homophobia. These interrelated attitudes all assume male superiority and female inferiority.

As Haney points out, the legacy we have received is that sexuality is viewed as a problem of control. According to her, sexual ethics traditionally proceeded from the belief that the essential human sexual nature includes two sexes and two genders that correspond to and are the opposite of each other. A powerful sexual force operates between the two sexes, and virtue requires that force to be controlled.

Legal and religious codes have long upheld heterosexual sex as the only morally permissible sexual relations, at least in part because of the emphasis placed on procreation in the traditional family. Men and women are described as complementary beings, needing one another in order to be complete and in order to further the human race. Any sexual act which goes against this is not only morally inferior, but a perversion of human nature itself. This understanding of human sexuality is reflected in the words of Jerry Falwell, the founder of the Moral Majority: "God Almighty created men and women biologically different and with differing needs and roles. He made men and women to complement each other and to love each other."[2] This point of view is also expressed in the slogan of the religious right: "God created Adam and Eve, not Adam and Steve." Western sexual ethics thus has both privileged heterosexuality and devalued gay and lesbian sexual selves. And, according to Haney, the primary agent for enforcing this value has been the "normative pattern of family organization . . . the nuclear family."[3]

More recently, however, religious ethicists and feminist theorists (both religious and secular) have challenged us to rethink our negative attitudes toward sexuality and spirituality. Much of this work has employed the term "embodiment," a recognition that as human beings we are embodied beings and cannot separate our physical existence from our spiritual. All human beings may have a soul, or a spiritual dimension, but as human beings we cannot know this part of ourselves divorced from our physical bodies. The part of Western Christianity which has proclaimed the subordination of the body to the soul as the paradigm of spiritual excellence denies that which makes spiritual awareness possible in this world, our flesh-and-blood existence. The newer approach, resting on the view that we are embodied beings, suggests that we cannot deny one part of ourselves for the sake of another, but must understand how spirit and body, soul and flesh are necessary components of a whole self.

In this sense, sexuality and spirituality are not antithetical, but rather are two of the most powerful and sacred expressions of an affirmation of human existence. Within both aspects we uncover the depths of ourselves, giving ourselves over wholly to a force that holds the potential for self-discovery and self-transcendence. Thus, for all persons, our understanding of ourselves as spiritual beings must incorporate who we are as sexual beings. Insofar as we can embrace our sexual identities we can most fully explore the dimensions of our spiritual possibilities.

The Erotic as More Than Genital Sex

In order to make the connection between our sexuality and our spirituality, it is necessary to expand our understanding of what it means to be a sexual being beyond genital sexual activity. We have found it useful to use the idea of the erotic as a means for exploration. While the term "erotic" certainly includes the possibility of physical sexuality, it encompasses much more than this. In her essay "Uses of the Erotic: The Erotic as Power," Audre Lorde defines the erotic as follows:

> The very word *erotic* comes from the Greek word *eros,* the personification of love in all its aspects—born of Chaos, and personifying creative power and harmony. When I speak of the erotic, then, I speak of it as an assertion of the lifeforce of women; of that creative energy empowered, the knowledge and use of which we are now reclaiming in our language, our history, our dancing, our loving, our work, our lives.[4]

Lorde is speaking about the experience of women, and speaking as a lesbian in particular. She argues that women have been oppressed in and through their bodies, and thus have been alienated from their own erotic power. We believe that Lorde's insights can be helpful in understanding gay men and lesbians insofar as we have also experienced oppression as the result of our identity. Lorde argues that oppressive systems must "corrupt or distort" all sources of power that are available to the oppressed class. When the erotic is distorted, when it is described as pornographic or perverted, it is difficult to claim it as a source of power. This corruption is necessary, says Lorde, to the maintenance of the oppressor's power, for it serves to suppress and control the oppressed.

The application of Lorde's insights to the lives of lesbians and gay men is illuminating. Certainly we can see how the distortion of homosexuality by the dominant social institutions (for example, religion, politics, the schools) has worked to devalue the lives of these men and women. Many of those we interviewed discussed their experiences as members of an oppressed class, and the ways in which this distorted their sense of self. According to Carla, a fifty-year-old lesbian, oppression cuts us off from one another:

> "I think lesbians are very isolated. That's part of our oppression: isolation. We are not mirrored back out in the culture. So we have to do that for each other. Even when you get the message 'Leave me alone.' "

A gay man in another group also discussed his sense of isolation as an adolescent and as a young man:

> "Withdrawing is somewhat typical of adolescence anyway, and boys tend to be more withdrawing. In general that happens to both gay and straight boys, but it seems like the gay boys like myself just withdrew and never came back. You got into the habit of not talking about your personal life in your teenage years, whereas heterosexual boys started talking when they were in college."

As both of these comments demonstrate, the inability to see oneself as accepted within society makes it extremely difficult to accept one's own identity, and therefore to have a self who can enter into relationships with others. If the only "natural" form of sexuality is heterosexuality, homosexual relations are deviant, and there is nothing to learn from them except perhaps a lesson in what not to be or do. So straight persons do not value the relationships of homosexuals in the same way that they value their own and can discount them as abnormal, "poor substitutes for the real thing." And gay men and lesbians, living in a heterocentric culture, internalize the same message.

In the course of our interviews, Hannah revealed that her own process of coming out was, first and foremost, a struggle to accept herself as a lesbian:

> "I knew I was a lesbian for a while, though I didn't use that word, I just couldn't. I thought that if I was a lesbian then I would end up alone and miserable in life; I thought I would end up an alcoholic, living in the gutter, without friends or family. Even though that was what I thought would happen, finally I could no longer pretend to be someone I wasn't. But I was really scared."

Clearly, if one lives with this kind of fear and self-hatred, there is little possibility for any sense of personal power. Later in the conversation, Hannah observed that internalized self-hatred affected not only individuals, but the whole gay and lesbian community:

> "We're an oppressed group of people, and I think that causes additional problems with being couples or not being couples, or sustaining long-term relationships. I think it's clear in racial minority communities as well, the same kinds of problems with self-worth and self-esteem, and hence in relating to other people on a long-term basis."

In response to our own conflicts of identity, we may be led to believe that the best we can do is to imitate heterosexual models as the morally superior mode of interaction. In so doing we are disempowered, because we are cut off from the very source of power that may provide our deepest resource. If we were actually to tap into our erotic power as a source for being in the world, we would not settle for or participate in our own oppression.

Feminist theologian Rita Brock explores the dimensions of erotic power as a theological category, contrasting *agape* (disinterested or objective love, often theologically defined as the love of God) with *eros,* which she defines as "intimacy through subjective engagement of the whole self in a relationship."[5] She claims that the erotic "bridges the passions of our lives by a sensual span of physical, emotional, psychic, mental, and spiritual elements."[6] The erotic, says Brock, is a love that is directed both to ourselves and to persons to whom we are related. It is the power that connects us to embodied others, that allows us to make empathic connections with others, that empowers us to have a hunger for justice in society. Such erotic power emerges from within oneself. Only when one accepts oneself for who she or he is and gains a sense of personal empowerment can erotic power manifest itself in our lives.

We want to consider Brock's model of erotic power in light of lesbian and gay experiences. On the one hand, we find limitations in her contention that the first place where we may feel erotic power is in our families of origin. It is here, says Brock, where we first experience interrelatedness and intimacy, and therefore feel the sense of connectedness to others which is the key to erotic power.[7] Yet, as we have observed, biological families may also be the place where we lesbians and gay men feel most disconnected from ourselves because of our sexuality. Because, as Brock argues, the erotic involves the "subjective engagement of the whole self in a relationship," the necessity to hide a significant part of ourselves from our families makes such engagement difficult, if not impossible.

Two gay men discussed the fact that although their families knew they were gay, their partners were never acknowledged for "who they really are." One of the men expressed resentment toward his parents, but the other man challenged this:

> "In turn, you've never acknowledged this, and said this is my lover whom I sleep with, who's my life partner, whom I'm romantically involved with."
>
> "Right, but it's not like they wouldn't know."
>
> "But they'd rather not know."

In contrast, then, to Brock's model, in which biological families teach about erotic power, our biological family relations may break our hearts the most.

Our gay/lesbian families, on the other hand, can be the place where we are renewed and restored, where erotic power is nurtured in the same fashion that Brock ascribes to biological families. It is here that we are known and accepted for who we are, including our sexual selves. This occurs not only in our most intimate partnerships, but also with our extended lesbian and gay kin.

A focus group of single lesbians and gay men discussed the ways in which their chosen families provided many of the things commonly associated with intimate partnerships. For example, part of the reason Kevin and Nathan share a home is that they are brothers, but both said adamantly that if they were not both gay, the kinship relationship would not be sufficient reason for them to be roommates. Kevin described what it was he valued about his relationship with his brother:

> "I have almost everything in a partner except the romantic relationship. I have that bond, I have somebody to come home to. He has his nights out, I have my nights out, we have our nights out together. I know there are roommate relationships where they are at that level, yet it's not a sexual relationship. I think that living together creates a lot of that bond, because you do deal with what a mess you left in the sink, where you left your mail, what color your laundry was."

Here we have an example of erotic power and connection that is characterized by deep intimacy and love, and that includes and incorporates the sexuality of these two men but does not include sexual intimacy.

Hannah agreed that this kind of affection did not require a partner. She explained that she had a group of friends who shared a house where she found that kind of familial warmth:

> "I can just hang out there, which is really nice for me. It's more of family kinds of things. I can go there and I will get a lot of hugs, I will get kisses, I will get a lot of hanging out and working on projects together."

Here, again, erotic power can flourish in acts of affection and shared work that happen outside sexual relations. Yet, at the same time, Hannah's sexuality is not denied or devalued.

Both Audre Lorde and Rita Brock identify the erotic as a source of power that celebrates our physical, sexual selves but is not limited to our sexuality. Lorde speaks of it as a "lifeforce"; Brock describes it as that which "bridges the passions of our lives." Erotic power is found in the freedom to be open to ourselves and to others in all the dimensions of our lives. It is that which inspires us to sing, and to dance, to laugh out loud, to be totally outrageous—and to invest our passions and our joys in all aspects of our lives and work.

The concrete acts of love we show our gay/lesbian family members help to nurture them and renew them. Incarnate love is erotic power in action. Once again, these acts of love demonstrate the reality of our relationships, they reinforce the intimacy of gay/lesbian kinship over time. The power and passion of erotic love is really the force guiding the other values we have articulated. Erotic power makes possible a world where, as Sandra Golvin poetically phrased it, "fun, hot, sexy, and profoundly moral all mean the same thing."

Part 2

Creating New Meanings

7

Marriage and Family

•→ The Rancho is a restaurant and banquet facility that specializes in weddings. On a particular spring day one ceremony is in progress, a man and woman joining their lives in marriage. Across the open courtyard another ceremony is about to begin. Two clergy come forward. A pianist begins to play a song, and a friend of the couple begins to sing. At the top of the stairs a teenage boy and girl link arms and begin to march toward the altar. Behind them is a young man holding two wedding rings. These are the children of the two people who will join their lives today; both had been married previously. As family and friends look to the top of the stairs, Barb and Sandy smile broadly. They both hold bouquets of flowers and descend the staircase arm in arm.

This is a blessing of a union between two women who wish to share their lives with each other. All the elements that our culture associates with weddings are present: flowers, candles, music, the blessing of religious leaders. After the ceremony all the guests celebrate with a champagne toast, a wedding cake, and plenty of food. This indeed is a celebration of life. Yet, this ceremony on a beautiful spring day in California also raises questions. Is it too much like a heterosexual wedding? Are these two women trying to fit themselves into wedding garments that were made for others to wear?

Jesus told his disciples a parable: "No one tears a piece from a new garment and sews it on an old garment; otherwise the new will be torn, and the piece from the new will not match the old. And no one puts new wine into old wineskins; otherwise the new wine will burst the skins and will be spilled, and the skins will be destroyed" (Luke 5:36–37).

Which Is the Real Family?

We have argued, along with many other feminist, lesbian, and gay critics, that the traditionalist model of the standard American family neglects the concerns and experiences of significant portions of society at best, and is exclusionary and oppressive at worst. As a result, gay men and lesbians find no easy answers when they attempt to define and name their intimate relationships in light of the family mystique that is dominant in our society. In contemporary society the term family is linked to biological relationships and to heterosexual marriage to such a degree that any other form seems mimetic, a representation of the "real" family that doesn't quite fit. Using terms such as marriage and family becomes problematic for some gay men and lesbians because they feel that these words are too heavily laden with heterosexual meaning. Can we stretch the concepts of marriage and family to include new family forms, or will we simply tear the cloth and burst the wineskins?

A question central to this debate is whether any one form of marriage and family fits the definition of a "real" family. Which is mimetic reflection? The terms family and marriage are themselves linguistic representations of a structure/system that exists in the real world. Alternative forms of family and marriage already exist in the real world, but in some sense they have to be set in contrast to the traditional model. So, for example, discussions about "single-parent families" continue to privilege the notion that "real" families have two parents. The identification of "female-headed households" sets these apart from "real" households headed by males. Despite the fact that many families and households lack two parents and nevertheless function as families within society, our culture continues to discuss these as if they were aberrations. In the end, it seems there is no single "real" family. Even those that are more or less traditional are representations of a model, an image that only takes on flesh when real people give it validity in their lives. Canonizing a certain form of family as normative and investing it with certain social privileges is an issue of power, not of an ontological reality called *the family*.

Partnerships as Marriage?

Many of the men and women we interviewed believed that their inability to participate in the social ritual of marriage made it difficult for straight society to understand that their relationships constitute a family. As one lesbian in her forties, who is in a long-term relationship, reflected:

> "We don't have that demarcating event. We live together—like straight men and women live together—but they are not 'family' because they haven't had that marriage in front of everyone else. None of us have that demarcation, and maybe that's what's keeping others from looking at us as a family, because our culture has said that the family unit begins when you get married."

A single gay man made the point that, because he wasn't married, his parents did not perceive him as fully adult with a life of his own:

> "There is a map for families. When they get married and start having their own kids, it's okay to say, 'We're not coming home for Christmas.' But that doesn't happen to us, we don't make that transition as easy."

In mainstream American culture marriage and the nuclear family have become the taken-for-granted form of family with which lesbians and gay men must interact so as to be understood. Though we are denied participation in the institution of marriage, we nevertheless find ourselves bound by the linguistic conventions of society in attempting to make our lives intelligible. What we mean by this might be clarified by an analogy drawn from literary criticism.

Charles Eric Reeves, in a discussion of representation and mimesis, suggests that literary texts are not definitive representations of reality but rather representations of the many and various experiences of reality. Nevertheless, texts follow patterns and expectations in order to make representation intelligible. Changes within literary traditions are only understood against the backdrop of cultural consensus.[1] New literary representations are perceived as exceptional only because a convention already exists. In the same way, when lesbians and gay men talk about marriage and family, we do so in order to render our experiences intelligible to ourselves and our society. We are thus engaged not in a process of mimicking an existing model, but in weaving a new complexity by interacting with the tradition.

Much of the debate within the gay and lesbian communities has centered on the desirability of affirming our partnerships as marriages, having ceremonies of union to acknowledge them, and working in the legal and political arenas to gain recognition of such unions by the state. Are such attempts yet another way gay men and lesbians are being coopted and assimilated into the status quo? Or will our families and partnerships change the social institutions of marriage and family? Such questions raise both legal and social issues.

Law professor Paula Ettelbrick maintains that participation by lesbians and gay men in the institution of marriage will not challenge the existing social structures. Rather, she argues, it will make lesbians and gay men invisible, by assimilating the sexual liberation of lesbians and gay men within the heterosexist paradigm. According to Ettelbrick, "Marriage runs contrary to two of the primary goals of the lesbian and gay movement: the affirmation of gay identity and culture and the validation of many forms of relationships."[2] Gay and lesbian sex outside the context of a marriage would, she feels, be further stigmatized. Ettelbrick does not discount the positive legal benefits that accrue to those who are married. Instead, she argues, legal recognition of all kinds of domestic partnerships is a more worthy goal because it allows for the diversity of family networks to emerge in the context of gay and lesbian experience.

While Ettelbrick's argument seeks to extend legal recognition and benefits to a greater variety of familial relations, it may place an undue burden on the gay and lesbian community. It asks that a group of persons who are already marginalized and stigmatized lead the charge, so to speak, for the reformation of a dominant social institution. It seems unlikely, at this point in time, that extending domestic partnership status to gays and lesbians will do much to dismantle the privilege accorded to married persons.

This sentiment is reflected by attorney Thomas Stoddard in his arguments in favor of gay marriage. While Stoddard is critical of marriage as a traditional heterosexual, and often heterosexist, institution, he maintains that legal recognition of lesbian and gay marriages is an important goal for the gay and lesbian civil rights agenda. Legal protection would allow partners to reduce tax liability, gain governmental spousal benefits, and inherit from each other without a will. These and other economic and legal incentives are necessary for improving the social status of lesbians and gay men. "Marriage is much more than a relationship sanctioned by law," he writes. "It is the centerpiece of our entire social structure, the core of the traditional notion of 'family.' "[3]

Opening the institution of marriage to same-sex relationships, Stoddard argues, would do much to bring about societal acceptance of gay men and lesbians because this central social relationship would be transformed to include another way of being married. In contrast, domestic partnership ordinances convey another image—that same-sex relationships are somehow less valuable than heterosexual marriages, that gay men and lesbians are incapable of being "really" married.

In addition to giving societal value to gay/lesbian relationships, enlarging the concept of marriage to include gay men and lesbians would transform the institution itself by questioning the sexist assumptions inherent in the current construction of marriage. Feminist critics have long pointed out that the traditional marriage structure creates inequitable power relations by assigning leadership and authority to the husband/father. As law professor Nan Hunter has said, "Legalizing lesbian and gay marriage would have tremendous potential to destabilize the gendered definition of marriage."[4]

The Larger Political Battle

In that they have provided some small recognition of same-sex relationships, domestic partnerships have been a valuable temporary solution. They are, however, a stage toward the larger goal of full recognition in marriage. Gay men and lesbians who argue for domestic partnership as an end in itself are settling for a two-tier system of separate and not equal recognition of their unions. William N. Eskridge holds that we ought not to settle for anything less than full participation. Marriage as an exclusively heterosexual institution, he writes, "is the most blatant evidence that gay and lesbian citizens must sit in the back of the law bus."[5]

Clearly, the legal and political battle with regard to same-sex marriage continues to rage. On September 10, 1996, the U.S. Senate passed the Defense of Marriage Act, which prohibits the federal government from recognizing same-sex marriages and allows individual states to refrain from recognizing them. President Clinton signed the bill into law on September 21, 1996.[6] The Defense of Marriage Act emerged as a response to the recent court battles in the state of Hawaii. Three same-sex couples filed a lawsuit against the state of Hawaii claiming that current marriage laws preventing same-sex couples from marrying violated the couples' right to privacy and equal protection.

Even though the case was dismissed in trial court, the Hawaii State Supreme Court held that the case had merit and should be heard because the current law does violate equal protection under the state's constitution. On December 3, 1996, the judge ruled that the state of Hawaii must issue marriage licenses to the three couples because the state had provided no compelling reasons to deny them. The case is now on appeal. In the meantime, Hawaii has passed a law that establishes "reciprocal beneficiaries"; for a fee of eight dollars same-sex couples may receive a state certificate qualifying them for many legal rights and benefits usually reserved for married persons. While some persons see this as a positive step toward recognizing same-sex relationships, others argue that it is a conservative move to continue to protect marriage as a heterosexual-only institution.

Whatever the outcome in the Hawaii case, it is clear that the case will not be resolved quickly. In reaction, Congress introduced the Defense of Marriage Act to block immediate recognition of same-sex marriages performed in Hawaii should the courts find in favor of the couples' case. The Defense of Marriage Act adds language to current federal law specifically stating that no state or territory shall be required to acknowledge marriage between two people of the same sex if such a marriage is acknowledged in another state. Further, the act defines marriage as "a legal union between one man and one woman as husband and wife."[7] Those in favor of the act have argued that broadening the definition of marriage to include same-sex unions "would threaten the special legal, social, and economic status of the traditional heterosexual family."[8]

Clearly, if same-sex marriages were recognized, heterosexual marriages would no longer enjoy special status. It remains unclear, however, in what way acknowledging same-sex unions as marriages threatens the heterosexual family itself. Rights are not like sale items at a department store which are limited in number and, once gone, no longer available. It seems to us that giving equal rights to same-sex couples simply gives everyone equal opportunity.

Many conservatives argue that gay men and lesbians are arguing for so-called special rights when they seek antidiscrimination laws. But the Defense of Marriage Act seems to advocate special rights for heterosexual persons and to discriminate against the equal rights of gay men and lesbians to pursue their happiness in marrying someone they love. Despite recent anti–affirmative action sentiment, it appears that special privileges based on sexuality are still permissible.

In discussing the legalization of gay marriage, Andrew Sullivan questions why even political conservatives would not support it. In marriage, two people make a deeper commitment to each other than they do by simply living together. "Conservatives should not balk at the apparent radicalism of the change involved," he writes.

> The introduction of gay marriage would not be some sort of leap in the dark, a massive societal risk. Homosexual marriages have always existed in varying forms; they have just been euphemized. Increasingly they exist in every sense but the legal one. . . . It could bring the essence of gaylife—a gay couple—into the heart of the traditional family in a way the family can most understand and the gay offspring can most easily acknowledge. It could do more to heal the gay–straight rift than any amount of gay rights legislation.[9]

Sullivan's argument moves beyond the legal questions about gay and lesbian marriage to address the social implications that underlie the judicial concerns. Many gay men and lesbians believe that participating in the institutions of marriage and family will help straight people understand that we are not defined solely by our sexuality. We are, after all, products of this society, and thus many in our communities share in the desire to share love in a relationship of commitment, although not all lesbians and gay men are in agreement about the value of gay/lesbian marriage.

Ken, one of the single gay men we interviewed, explained it like this:

> "Well, I think there's what I call the forever myth. I mean it's in every pop song, every country song, every movie you watch, and every book you read that there's supposed to be one and only one person that you're supposed to hook up with and it's supposed to be hunky-dory and everybody's supposed to live happily ever after. And if you don't do it then you're a half-person; you're less than a full person. And I don't feel I get it any stronger or any less strong from my gay friends than I do from anyone else; it just permeates everything."

Clearly, for Ken this is a myth that is problematic. Yet, another single man in the same focus group saw it as more than simply a socially constructed myth. According to him:

> "It is a basic human need, that bonding, that closeness. [Not having] that physical closeness is the hard part; that's the thing that I can't deal with. That warmth, that other life next to you. That's the hardest part I have in being single."

Bruce Bawer argues that gay marriage has important personal and political impact. Bawer maintains that creating a family of two, creating a home, and living life together is an extension of the coming-out process. He points out that creating a self-identity as gay does not necessarily mean fully integrating one's sexual orientation into the whole of one's life. It is possible to compartmentalize the sexual self from other aspects of one's identity, and many gay men and lesbians know the experience of living this kind of fragmented existence.

Bawer argues that having a committed relationship suddenly brings up issues heterosexuals must address. A gay man in a relationship must confront a moral question concerning what he will say to co-workers and family about his partner. Being open about relationships also requires straight people to confront the reality of gay men's lives. According to Bawer, this challenges their compartmentalization of gay men's sexual selves as a "dirty little secret."[10] As we discussed in chapter 4, the gay and lesbian parents we interviewed came to a similar conclusion as a result of their experiences of confronting straight people with their identity as both parents and as gay men or lesbians.

Some of those we interviewed said that they felt pressure, from both gay and straight friends, to find a life partner. Jenny, a bisexual woman, acknowledged that her friends exerted subtle forms of pressure on her:

> "Most of my friends here are married heterosexuals, so there is a little bit of pressure. They don't care what sex the person is, but there is a little bit of pressure that they don't want me to be alone all of the time."

A gay man in his forties agreed with her:

> "I get it more from my heterosexual colleagues than I do from my gay friends. Every one of my heterosexual colleagues is constantly asking me about finding a person, wanting me to bring a date to their dinner parties. I think it's partly because they don't understand the concept of friendship in the way that we do, in the sense that for us it's often a very important source. A lot of my heterosexual colleagues don't seem to have that, especially the men; they have a very narrow range, virtually no friends. I think it's also a concern that you're not alone, because for them coupleness is the only alternative to aloneness."

Another single gay man, Tom, understood this pressure differently:

> "There's not a pressure, but there's a desire. I'm fairly religious; I think God put us here initially to mate and procreate. Well, to me, there's enough people now, so what's left is to mate. Every person should have someone."

Clearly, among the men and women we interviewed, there is no consensus about the value of marriage as a political or social goal. Tom observed that a political element exists in the gay community that is against the entire matter. Kevin responded that although he wasn't against gay marriage, he felt too much emphasis was being placed on this issue:

> "I don't think that this ought to be a major political issue—gay marriages—on the political agenda. I don't like that as a top priority."

Some voices within the lesbian and gay community, like Kevin's, have resisted the move to accept the marriage model. Many of those we spoke with believed that an emphasis on marriage would tend to isolate single persons. They reflected that, as a whole, society tends to value single people less than couples, and they did not want to see the gay and lesbian communities move in this direction. Hannah, a single lesbian in her forties, expressed this point of view:

> "I do think there's a lot more acceptance of people being single in the gay community than in the straight community. My straight friends are sorely put upon by their friends, are regularly 'set up' on blind dates because straight married people in particular don't want their single friends by themselves. I think they're somewhat threatened."

Kevin, a single gay man, concurred:

> "They can't do 'couples' things; they're always a third wheel."

Hannah agreed, commenting that she did not feel this way in the gay community.

In another focus group, a single gay man observed that couples tend to withdraw from communities:

> "I see my gay friends who go into couples as being very isolated, and not always interacting with friends, and that can be the dynamics of a couple independent of being gay or straight."

Thus, one of the concerns with gay marriage is that gay men and lesbians will follow the pattern of the heterosexual nuclear family that withdraws into itself, away from a broader community. For gays and lesbians this is a particular concern, since the gay community has been so important as a source of support and identity. Sandy, one of the four lesbians who share a home, said part of the reason they made this decision to live as a family unit was because she and her partner did not want to be isolated as a couple:

> "I think that when there are just two, just a couple, there is the issue of isolation. It is harder to maintain and rear a family with just the two of us. My experience is that with four of us it feels more like a unit, like a unified presence. There are all of these other possibilities for relationship, and things get dealt with differently than when there are only two people."

Other men and women we interviewed, while they agreed that these concerns were significant, felt that support for couples and the recognition of same-sex marriages were nevertheless important. The following conversation emerged in a group of single men and women who wrestled with the question of gay marriage and its implications.

> "Do you think the fact that, as gay people, we can't get officially, legally married, makes it a lot easier to just dump it when you get tired of it?"
>
> "I think so. I mean there's no financial connection, there's not any sanctity of society and all that hoopla that goes along with weddings."
>
> "There's no real bind, no ritual and bonds."
>
> "We never had good role models; maybe that's part of the problem we have been talking about. We don't have a good role model for what is a good [gay] marriage, what is a good, healthy, strong, well-functioning marriage."
>
> "You don't have an Ozzie and Harriet . . ."

There are no easy answers to the question of gay and lesbian marriage. There are compelling arguments on both sides of the issue. We understand the reticence of some members of the gay and lesbian communities to see marriage as a goal in the movement for liberation. We know that forms of family exist that do not fit into the marriage model. We also believe in promoting the diversity of various family forms. At the same time, we believe that those homosexual couples who want to enter into a covenant of committed love should be able to do so with all the benefits that heterosexual couples receive. Those who do not want to undertake this form of commitment should not be coerced into doing so, but neither should those who wish to make the commitment be made to feel guilty or that they have somehow "sold out."

Some people may argue that the social, economic, and legal privileges accorded to married persons by society are a recognition of the value of a committed relationship and the effort invested to sustain such relationships. Whether these people are gay or straight, the commitment and the effort are the same and should be equally valued. However, others question the justice of granting such privileges to married couples, whether gay or straight. Why should a childless married couple, for example, receive tax incentives not given to single persons? Critics suggest that such privileges are a way of reinforcing the status quo by encouraging people to marry and procreate. Should not the commitments of those who dedicate their lives to children as teachers, but who do not marry, also receive recognition for their contributions? While gay men and lesbians fight to have their partnerships given equal acknowledgment under the law, these broader issues of justice cannot be ignored.

The fact that two people have made a public commitment to each other does not make the relationship or the marriage, yet the experience of a ritual that cements a bond already existing between the partners can alter the way in which a couple experiences the relationship. On the evening of their wedding day, Barb and Sandy sat on a hilltop overlooking the Pacific Ocean. They told us that, as they watched the sunset that day, they felt that something spiritual had happened to them. In some way they were changed by the experience of standing before their friends and family and making a public commitment to love each other. The question of whether or not society will some day recognize this relationship remains unanswered.

(Re)Politicizing the Family

•➤ Now a man's house ought to be the beginning, or rather a small component part of the city. . . . Domestic peace contributes to the peace of the city . . . [because this] . . . contributes to the ordered harmony concerning authority and obedience obtaining among the citizens.

—St. Augustine, *The City of God*

Indeed, the family is a civil society established by Nature: this society is the most natural and the most ancient of all societies; it serves as a foundation for the national society; for a people or a nation is nothing more than an entirety compounded of several families.

—Chevalier de Jaucourt, *Encyclopédie ou dictionnaire raisonné des sciences, des arts et métiers*

The marriage bond has been recognized in Judeo-Christian tradition as well as in the legal codes of the world's most advanced societies as the cornerstone on which society itself depends for its moral and spiritual rejuvenation, as that culture is handed down father to son, mother to daughter.

—Senator Robert Byrd, quoted in the *San Francisco Chronicle*

"And every one who has left houses or brothers or sisters or father or mother or children or lands, for my name's sake, will . . . inherit eternal life."

—Jesus of Nazareth, Matthew 19:29

Alternative Family Values as Social Goods

To this point, we have considered the family and our interactions within it, suggesting new models for transforming our intimate relationships. We have argued that such transformation is necessary for the creation of less oppressive family systems. We now wish to turn our attention to the broader social sphere, for it is our contention that alternative family values are necessary not only within our interpersonal relations, but also for the creation of the good society.

Without attending to this question, it is possible that a reader might reflect, "Well, that is all well and good—you adopt *your* model of family, but I'll stick with my own." Readers can too easily conclude that family systems are simply a matter of personal choice. We want to claim much more than this, namely, that the family is a political institution.To do so, we will briefly revisit some of our earlier discussions in a consideration of how traditional family values affect us not only as individual members of families but also as members of the body politic.

The family has been described, historically and in contemporary discussions, by both conservatives and progressives alike, as the fundamental unit or building block of society. Claims are made that if the family is in disarray, so is society, and such claims are not new. These arguments date back at least to the time of Aristotle, who maintained that the family or household existed to serve the needs of the state. Augustine also asserted that civic peace and stability were secured first by domestic peace. These attitudes continued throughout the Middle Ages. Enlightenment thought, which challenged the divine right of kings and proclaimed the rights of the individual, continued to espouse the importance of the family for the well-being of the political sphere. Though Enlightenment thinkers argued for the privatization of the family, this did not preclude their understanding of the family as the basic unit of society.

This association of familial stability with political stability continues to the present day and is one of the much-repeated arguments in the "culture war" that is currently being waged. We have been told, for example, that when women left the home in large numbers to enter the workforce, a host of social problems were unleashed—including juvenile delinquency, teenage pregnancy, gang violence, and drug abuse. These and many other contemporary crises are blamed on the erosion of traditional family roles.

As we have observed, the "traditional" family of late-twentieth-century U.S. culture is not so traditional, being a relatively new arrival in the history of family systems. Whereas earlier philosophers and theologians made explicit the relation between the state and the household, and were not timid in claiming that the family existed for the good of the state, our contemporary understanding of family is much more complex—the modern family is characterized by privatization and individualism.

Given this understanding, the general consensus is that the state should not interfere in the private lives of citizens, nor should individual interests be subsumed under the political demands of the state, except perhaps in times of extreme urgency, such as war. The service the family owes to the state is not so blatantly identified. Rather, the family is seen as the place in which particular virtues or values are to be learned, virtues that translate into good citizenship and consequently to a good society.

We should note that this understanding of the relation of family and state is an ideological construction, one that does not necessarily reflect the realities of many persons who live within both traditional and not-so-traditional families. Nevertheless, this is the ideology that functions within the American political debate over the family, and this ideology creates the paradoxical relationship of family and state in the contemporary arena. Our political system is premised on the primacy of individual rights. Citizens are individuals who agree to abide by the rule of the state. They relinquish certain individual rights in exchange for protection, by the state, of more fundamental rights. So, for example, we agree not to drive as fast as we want whenever we want, and, in exchange, the government enforces traffic laws to help ensure our safety on the highways.

In this model, then, the state serves the individual, not the other way around. Nevertheless, political argument continues to insist that, ultimately, this is for the good of the state. If the state comprises individuals, then insofar as individual rights are secured and protected, the state is stable and flourishes. The rationale behind this is not that the state has primacy, but that the individual does. This is one of our most cherished political convictions and the basis of our understanding of civil rights. It is not our intent to argue against the primacy of individual rights, but rather to point out the paradoxical problem in claiming that individuals ought to care about the body politic while at the same time claiming that the body politic merely serves an instrumental purpose in relation to individual citizens.

The understanding of the family as a private unit, and the separation of the public and private spheres of endeavor that characterizes U.S.

political and social life, means that the family has effectively withdrawn from the body politic. The family unit is disconnected and unresponsive to the needs of society since those needs are not ultimately understood to make claims upon the family.

Although we are supposed to learn the virtues/values of good citizens within the family structure, what we are actually taught is that as individuals our needs come first, that certain persons within the family are more powerful than others, and that this is the natural state of affairs. After the needs of individuals, the needs of the family come next. Our family unit has primacy over our neighbors or more distant others within our communities. Finally, the state may make claims on us only when it is to the direct advantage of the individuals sheltered within the family.

The securing of individual rights, and the corresponding rise to social dominance of the nuclear family, created an ideology in which the state is understood to be suspect. It is taken as truth that the state must be guarded against, and that the individual and the state must have a relationship characterized by antagonism. The question that must be asked is how the family can create citizens who will be invested in the creation of the "good society" when our fundamental ideology is that society—the political state—is at best a necessary evil.

We would argue that this antagonism is not necessary, but is the result of particular social, economic, philosophical, and theological developments. The time has come, we believe, to rethink these developments and the values that have arisen as a result. We do not wish to jettison claims for individual rights, but rather to expand our understanding of the individual and the location of the individual within a community. We become individuals not in isolation but in a community of other individuals. The understanding that individualism cannot be secured except within community must receive attention in discussions of the relation of family and state. We believe that the experiences of lesbians and gay men provide a model for such a reconceptualization.

Ultimately, it seems to us that what is required is a repoliticization of the family, a rethinking of the relationship between the family and the state and of the role of the family in creating citizens of the state. For if, as many theorists have argued, we do learn our earliest lessons in citizenship within the family system, then we need to seriously attend to what we are learning from our traditional family values.

We disagree with those who claim that the social problems we now confront have arisen because families have stopped teaching traditional family values. Rather, we maintain that traditional family values are not able to address the problems of contemporary society. Thus, a return to traditional values would not cure our social ills. The prescription is a new value system, one that recognizes that the world continues to change. We offer our system for discussion and consideration.

Traditional Family Values and Citizenship

It is no great insight to observe that proponents of traditional family values appear to be caught up in a romantic nostalgia for a perceived golden age, whether or not that age was as golden as it is made out to be. Most critics of this nostalgia observe that the golden age appears to have been somewhere around the late eighteenth to early nineteenth century. This is the time in which middle-class sensibilities rose to social dominance, and the image of the nuclear family became the cultural ideal. The values attached to this family model were thus part and parcel of white middle-class experience, and served to reinforce this experience as the societal norm.

These values, however, were also derived from earlier social systems. Specifically, they were part of the cultural and religious legacy inherited by the nineteenth-century United States. So-called traditional family values must be understood in terms of their historical rootedness as well as their culturally specific location. Taking both these considerations into account, it seems to us that the time has come to rethink what is valuable about these traditional family values. These values might have worked, at one point in our history, to create the kinds of citizens necessary for what was conceived as "the good society," but contemporary understandings of the good society have changed. Correspondingly, the values we teach must also change.

The most fundamental and observable difference between then and now is that our society has become increasingly pluralistic. In the nineteenth century, most U.S. citizens could, if they chose, go throughout their lives without interacting with someone too terribly different from themselves. Communities were closely demarcated along religious, racial, and ethnic lines—lines that need not be crossed if one was in the position of social dominance. For those in a position of social subordination, the choice to cross such lines was often taken out of their hands; for example, a black slave could not choose whether or not to work for a white slave owner. Crossing the lines was, more often than not, understood to be undesirable, occasioned by necessity and avoided if possible. The nineteenth-century United States still operated on the maxim that persons should "stick with their own kind."

The late-twentieth-century United States is a horse of a different color. Yes, there are still those who believe that we are better off if we don't mix with those different from ourselves, but the boundaries along which difference is defined have become more fluid. According to one of the women we interviewed, a college professor and a lesbian:

> "My grandmother, for example, might have been willing to tolerate certain non-Methodist Protestants (Baptists and Presbyterians, for example, though Episcopalians were suspect), but she was sure that Roman Catholics were not Christian, and worshiped the Pope, and should be avoided whenever possible. Among the students I find in my classroom these days, such distinctions make little or no sense."

Today, most people find their lives characterized by a far greater diversity than our grandparents could have imagined or would have tolerated. Most people have friends of a different religion; some also have friends of different cultural or ethnic heritage. While racism continues to be a plague upon the land, most people would find it difficult to get through life without at some time sitting in a classroom, or working in a job, or going to a social event where persons of different races were not also present.

It is not simply in our schools and workplaces and social worlds that diversity has changed the character of our lives. The world has shrunk dramatically since our grandparents' day. We know, almost immediately, of events that occur thousands of miles away. We know the faces of the children in Bosnia. We know the celebrations and the struggle that occurred in South Africa. For those of us who lived through the earthquake in southern California in January 1994, the suffering of the citizens of Kobe, Japan, in January 1995 was tangible. We live in a world where, by virtue of rapidly changing technology, persons whose lives once seemed as different from ours as night from day now seem oddly familiar. Our tastes in music, art, literature, food have all diversified. The United States is no longer a homogenous society, and in all likelihood will never be so again.

The pluralism that characterizes our culture is also reflected in the variety of choices we are asked to make on a daily basis. Not only the mundane choices (like, do I want Mexican or Italian food for dinner,

Jamaican or German beer to go with it?), but the more serious choices as well. The variety of religious options available also means a variety of value systems to choose between, a variety of ethical codes by which to live one's life. The idea that our children will simply do as their parents have done, because "that's the way we've always done it," is far less likely.

Future generations will also have to make other kinds of choices that past generations never dreamed of—life-and-death choices brought about by rapidly changing medical technology, new advances in environmental science, advancing theories in physics. And they will have to make such choices in a world that gives them an increasing array of options to choose from. Tradition and habit just will not equip them for the world they are going to inherit.

Diversity is a fact of life for late-twentieth-century America, although the value of such diversity is still being debated. Unfortunately, traditional family values do little to equip our children to become responsible citizens in a pluralistic society. In earlier, homogeneous societies, characteristics necessary to the peaceful existence of the body politic were such things as obedience, unquestioned acceptance of authority (legitimated by appeals to natural law or divine authority), and distrust of those other than one's own (a fierce nationalism).

However, in a pluralistic society such as ours, we must ask whether these same values continue to serve the good of society or whether they may not, in fact, contribute to many contemporary social ills. Are such problems as an apathetic citizenry, the breakdown of communities, and increasing violence in the street and home the result of traditional values? If we continue to hold to values no longer appropriate and to teach them to our children, the future may be quite grim.

We want to make it clear that we do not categorically reject arguments made on behalf of the family and its importance to society. We agree with those who claim that the good society is determined by the character of its citizenry, and that persons learn their earliest lessons in citizenship within family structures. Thus, family values are critical to our future well-being.

We disagree, however, with those who champion traditional family values on three key issues: their definition of family, their concept of the good society, and their understanding of which values will best secure the future of society. We thus wish to consider our reconception of family values as we move from a discussion of individual families to concepts of community.

Before proceeding, it is necessary to say a few words about the terminology we will be using. In light of the diversity which characterizes our contemporary world, it seems to us that it is time to revisit the concept of democracy, the ideological foundation of U.S. politics. As an ideal system, democracy has much to recommend it. Consider the following dictionary definitions of democracy: "a system of government by the whole population . . . a classless and tolerant form of society."[1]

We are aware, however, that the democratic ideal has not always been realized in the history of the United States. Within a democracy, citizenship is required for participation, and access to citizenship is determined by those in power. Thus, although the Declaration of Independence affirmed in the eighteenth century that "all men are created equal [and] endowed . . . with certain inalienable rights," in practice this meant all free, white, property-owning males. Women and African Americans waited until the twentieth century for these inalienable rights to become a reality. The battle to extend civil rights to all members of society has been long and painful and is still being fought.

Despite the fact that actual democracy has not been a historical reality, the ideological strength of the word has masked the abuses of power that exist under this rubric. To invoke the word in an unreflective way is to risk perpetuating oppressive structures. Those who benefit from inequitable power structures may read the word assuming that we talk about the status quo, and conclude that this poses no critique of them. Those who are disenfranchised may also read this as "business as usual" and assume that we have nothing to offer.

As we consider our vision of the good society we nevertheless choose to make use of the word democracy, holding to the ideal while recognizing the problems inherent in the ideology. In so doing, we qualify the word with the antecedents "pluralistic" and "participatory" in the hope that this will provide a context for our understanding. Our vision of the good society is indeed a "classless and tolerant form of society," "a system of government by the whole population." A new social ethic is necessary for this to become a reality.

Let us now rethink (or redefine) the family values we examined in part 1.

A Broader Understanding of Fidelity

The value of fidelity, within traditional family values, has focused on the relationships of husbands and wives, and presumes that gender complementarity is natural: men and women are different beings, and each is incomplete without the other. This implies that neither can be fully a person without the other. Heterosexuality is presented as a necessary condition for the fulfillment of human nature. Further, within the traditionalist model, fidelity has to do with sexual practice. One is a faithful wife or husband if one does not violate the vow of sexual exclusivity made as part of the marriage contract.

We believe that the broader understanding of the value of fidelity that arises from the model of lesbian and gay families provides a model of faithfulness more appropriate to a pluralistic society. The model of fidelity we proposed in chapter 2 operates as a covenantal relationship. This model implies mutual obligation and responsibility without being act-specific, and implies authentic commitment between persons.

When fidelity is understood as a covenant between persons, the morality of our actions is determined by the quality of our relationships, not by adherence to a specific code of behavior. Friendship seems to us an apt model for considering this understanding of covenant. This is because friendships exist outside of legal and religious institutions and must struggle to survive without the support of such institutions. We do not have a ceremony, equivalent to marriage, for the taking of a best friend. We do not stand before God, state, and community and take vows of friendship. And yet, those of us who are fortunate enough to have someone we call our "best friend" know well that this is often the deepest and most lasting relationship of our lives.

The best friendships are those that allow for change and growth, that tolerate failure as well as celebrate success, where we can be both fragile and strong, lead as well as follow, and know that our friend will remain faithful to us (and we to them) through all the transitions. This faithfulness is premised on a commitment we have made to one another, a commitment that is continually remade as time and circumstance require, without any official rules or guidebooks as to how this is done. We remain friends not because of vows taken, or documents signed, but because we are committed to one another. One of the lesbians we interviewed described her relationship with her best friend as follows:

> "Mary and I have been best friends for more than twenty years. We have seen each other through marriages and divorces, deaths and births. We have gone through graduate school and career changes. We have struggled with our fears and celebrated our joys. We have sobbed in each other's arms, and laughed together until we were sick. She knows my darkest secrets, and I know hers, and we both know these secrets are safe. We have grown up together, and will grow old together. And through all the years,

no matter how badly I have screwed up, the one constant in my life is this: Mary loves me."

Fidelity understood as one model of covenantal relationship does not assign authority to one person and obedience to another. It does not assume that by divine or natural right one will lead and the other follow. It does not determine the morality of an action based on a preordained code of expectations.

It is possible that such an experience of fidelity can be found within heterosexual monogamous relationships (and in the best of marriages this is the case), but when it exists it is because both partners have gone beyond what is required by the marriage contract. However, fidelity understood as covenant can exist outside of marriage, and often does. It is not the fact of marriage that makes the covenant moral; it is the quality of the relationship.

We believe that the value of fidelity, redefined in this way, holds greater promise for the creation of responsible citizens in a pluralistic democracy. While still maintaining the value of commitment, it teaches us that commitments come in many forms and are not static. Authority may be wielded by anyone, and no one has a singular right to hold authority. Concomitant with authority is accountability to others, and we may lose authority if we are unwilling to be held accountable. Covenants are a two-way street; they are maintained only insofar as both (or all) parties involved continually renew their commitment to the well-being of both self and other.

The Moral Worth of Mutuality and Accountability

We have already pointed to some of the problems inherent in the traditional family values of unconditional love, duty, and obligation. We now wish to consider the question of how these translate into attributes of citizenship, and whether or not mutuality and accountability might better serve contemporary society.

Unconditional love, at its best, offers us a sense of security and acceptance. There is always a place to go home to. As we have seen, however, the requirement of unconditional love can also be oppressive. It requires that we love somebody even if they are not lovable, even if they do not deserve this love, simply because they are kin. It may mean that we sacrifice our own best interests for the sake of the family. It may mean that we abdicate our responsibility to others because the family requires it.

Ethicists Sarah Lucia Hoagland and Beverly Harrison have argued that the demand for unconditional love and the self-sacrifice it requires is usually a demand placed on the powerless by those in power. It is, all too often, rooted in inequitable power relations. We contend that the value of mutuality does not deny the possibility of loving others unconditionally, but it suggests that sacrifice for others must be entered into willingly and may not be imposed on less powerful members of society.

A consideration of this understanding of mutuality can be found in our earlier example of friendship. Friendships may be characterized by unconditional love and may exact sacrifice for others. However, such demands can be made only if the persons involved give assent. Friendships survive only as long as both parties remain committed to the continued significance of the relationship. It takes both people to be "best friends." We have all had the experience of seeing a friendship die out. For whatever reason, one person or the other, or perhaps both, gave up the commitment to sustaining the friendship. It cannot exist without both persons being present.

The concept of unconditional love, as an ongoing aspect of the family, is not rooted in the actual experience of relationships. Unconditional love is a false value which holds potential for damage. The requirement of unconditional love teaches us to suspend our moral sensibilities and our critical judgment in relationships.

If we must love unconditionally, it means that we must, at times, close our eyes to actions which do not deserve to be rewarded with love. Why must the abused wife continue to love her husband? Why must the child who has suffered incest continue to love Uncle Harold? Why must the brother continue to love his self-centered sibling? Simply because they are family? Common sense tells us no, and we would not continue friendships that were characterized by similar behaviors. Why must we accept this from family members?

In chapter 3 we recorded Kevin's thoughts about unconditional love; they bear repeating:

> "I am wondering about some people that I thought would be my extended group of friends forever who have slipped away. For some reason that wasn't unconditional. . . . I found that those relationships can be conditional . . . and that's something I'm struggling with right now."

Kevin told us that the conditional nature of relationships was something he had experienced not only with friends, but also with biological family members.

Family is neither good nor bad in itself; it is simply a relationship which we have invested with meaning over the centuries. It is a social, legal, and religious construct that recognizes kinship as one way of ordering our society. But this does not give it moral value. The value of family derives from the expectations, responsibilities, behaviors, and commitments that we invest in familial relationships. Devoid of these things, family has no more claim to moral worth than any other possible configuration we could imagine for the sustaining of human communities.

When we teach our children that family requires unconditional love, simply because it is family and for no other reason, we teach them that there are relationships which are above moral judgment. We teach them that some people do not have to be held accountable for their actions. In a pluralistic democracy this is a dangerous lesson.

There are many benefits that derive from pluralism, but there are also increasing challenges. There is more than one possible response to any given problem or question. There are a variety of options offered for dealing with social conflict. Choosing between such options requires discernment and critical evaluation of the possible courses of action. If we want our children to grow into responsible citizens, we need to begin by teaching them to engage in ethical decision-making. We do not do this by exempting certain relationships from moral judgment.

Unconditional love, coupled with the value of duty and obligation, sets individual interests against the social good. It further establishes obedience to authority as a good in and of itself. History is rife with those who have excused egregious behavior with the claim that "I was only following orders." More often than not, that excuse is not accepted. Yet this is precisely what we teach when we insist on unthinking loyalty as a demonstration of love. We fail to teach moral discernment to those from whom we would require it.

Duty for its own sake is not good unless the one to whom duty is owed is wholly good and without imperfection. Given the flawed and finite nature of human beings and the institutions we create, we cannot trust that mistakes will not be made. Thus, we must teach our children to be astute in their judgments, and this must begin in the family.

Mutuality as a form of relationship, rather than unconditional love, recognizes the importance of commitment. At the same time it does not exclude accountability and holds relationships answerable to a standard of justice. The standard of mutuality rejects the view that unjust power relations are normal and normative.

Mutuality also moves us away from an act-centered morality toward a relational ethic. Mutuality rests on the assumption that our actions are judged in the context of ongoing relationship in social as well as interpersonal relationships. As a social ethic, mutuality suggests that inequities between us must be continually open to critique and renegotiation in our common life together.

If we desire a society in which justice rules, then we must teach discernment at an early age. Whether we learn to be recipients of abuses of power or to be the perpetrators of them, we damage the social fabric as a whole when we accept such relationships as inevitable. Bullies are bullies because at some level they believe they have the right to impose their will on others. Victims become victims because they do not believe they have the right to say no and do not have faith that their refusal to be abused will be supported. Whether we are talking about schoolyard behavior or political machinations at the highest level does not matter. It is all of a piece. If we would live in a world without bullies or victims we must insist that blind obedience is owed to no one, and unchosen self-sacrifice is required of none.

Giving Life—A Larger Context

Traditional family values have included the celebration of reproduction within heterosexual marital monogamy. We do not wish to negate the importance of the bearing and rearing of children. Rather, we wish to expand the possibilities for how we re-create ourselves and the implications this has for a vision of the good society.

The emphasis on procreation/biological reproduction as the sole model for giving life is problematic in many ways. First, it invests biological relationships with value for their own sake: having children is a good thing simply because it is. The expectation for married couples is that they ought to reproduce, with very little consideration being given to why this is the case. Some will make reference to divine authority, as did Martin Luther, for example. For Luther, procreation was a direct command of God. Others will argue from nature; because one can reproduce, one ought to reproduce.

At this point in world history, we believe better reasons must be given for insisting on the value of biological reproduction. Environmentalists and futurists tell us that the earth has a dwindling supply of resources. Population control is a serious concern for those who advise zero population growth as a global commitment. Some worry about the impoverishment of developing countries and counsel population control, but do not concern themselves with more affluent countries. Others point to the inherent racism of such arguments about population control and argue instead that "first world" countries should stop ripping off the resources of "third world" countries via multinational corporations. Then, such proponents argue, they would have the resources to feed their people. While we believe such discussions are critically important, we do not engage them here.

Our concern is with the a priori assumptions placed on the value of procreation. Whatever stand one takes on the issue of population control, current realities require us to reexamine the high value we place on childbearing and challenge us to come up with good reasons for doing so. Obviously, if all women were to stop having children tomorrow, it would not be long before there was no younger generation to take on the responsibilities of society. For there to be a future there must be future generations. But this alone does not make childbearing a moral good.

Our concern here is to expand the possibilities for how we think about the value of the renewal and re-creation of society. We therefore point to a second problem with the privileging of biological parenthood. As we have discussed, the nuclear family turned inward upon itself, withdrawing from and setting itself over and against the broader society. Children were cherished and nurtured (at least ideally) within the nuclear family, and parents bore the responsibility for those children born to them. Other parents had the same obligation to their own children.

In this understanding of the family unit, the state was supposed to take a hands-off position in relation to parents and their children, except where parents were patently derelict in fulfilling the minimal obligations of providing food and shelter. What this often meant is that the more affluent members of society could expect minimal state interference, while the poorer members experienced greater state intrusion. There is a direct relation between economic security and the ability to live as private citizens.

In more recent years we have become aware of the fact that simply because a child is well fed and well clothed does not mean that the child is well cared for. In addition, as more and more families find themselves requiring two incomes for economic survival, even those we would consider relatively well-off find it increasingly difficult to adequately care for their children. For example, the lack of safe, affordable child care is gaining increasing attention as a serious social problem.

The privileging of biological reproduction and the privatization of the nuclear family have created a society that does not take seriously its obligation to the children of that society. Yes, we have public education, but those who can afford to do so opt out of this because our public education system is profoundly troubled. Yes, we have programs such as AFDC, and public health care, but welfare programs are under attack, and anyone who has ever sat in a health clinic knows that they are understaffed and the clients are underserved.

If we take seriously the value of fidelity previously discussed, we must ask what it means to be faithful to future generations. What is the meaning of covenant in relation to the society of which we are a part? How can we teach ourselves and our children responsibility to society when traditional family values teach us that we are accountable only to ourselves? Many would say, "I would like to provide for all children, but I can't afford to take care of my own." If we committed to caring for all children, our own would be included in this.

In a focus group of single gay men and lesbians, the participants reflected on their responsibility to future generations. As one lesbian expressed it:

> "Our biggest problem in society is that we as a culture, an American culture, have not cared for children the way we should. We have abused them, and taught them to be violent, and denied them an education. And they all need to be taken care of, they all need good role models. In the gay community this is an important job that needs to be done."

Because we have attached moral value to procreation only within heterosexual marital relationships, children born outside such relationships are less valued by society. Historically, "good" children were children who had identifiable fathers, and children who did not were social outcasts. Though popular culture is more tolerant these days of children born outside such unions, our legal and social systems are not so forgiving.

The lesson that may be learned from the experiences of lesbians and gay men is that family can be more than biological, and that the renewal and re-creation of society goes beyond parenting. Many of us have lost our biological families in the process of finding ourselves. If family were only biologically possible we would be orphans.

Fortunately, as we have discovered in our conversations with gay men and lesbians, biological relationship is not the only basis for family. We enter into covenantal relations to be family to one another. Allan, a single gay man, explains his understanding of family:

> "I think what I'm seeing, and what we are talking about, is that as we grow up we form our own families because we may not have necessarily gotten what we needed from our nuclear family. Family means being there for each other. I have just magnified that with my circle of friends. Family means having people around who support you."

Within our chosen families, we share resources, provide both emotional and economic support, celebrate holidays and mark passages in our lives. Like all families we sometimes argue, and cry, and laugh. We have found brothers and sisters, grandparents, aunts and uncles, and even parents. And we do this without the benefit of biological connection. Our experiences in making families have taught us that our responsibilities cross lines of nature to an extended network of others. In this sense, our families are always rooted in community.

Of course there are similar experiences in the heterosexual community. Many straight people, upon reading this, would probably say, "But I have that too!" The difference is that, for gay men and lesbians, this tends to be a common experience rather than an exceptional one. For those of us cut off from our biological families, in whole or in part, there is no other option. We must make our chosen families work because we cannot retreat to the biological family. For Hannah, one of the lesbians we interviewed, this consciousness about how we make family was one of the things she valued about the gay community.

> "I think we're better than straight people. We have to overcome certain things that they never have to deal with. They never have to look inside themselves and make decisions and deal with the kinds of stuff that we have to deal with."

There is an intentionality about our process of making family that may not exist in biological kinships. This gives us, perhaps, a more profound awareness of our connection with and responsibility to others within our communities, a sense of accountability to future generations who belong to us all.

Identity and Community—Celebrating Difference

Problems with traditional assumptions about identity and community, and our suggestions for a more nuanced understanding of this value, have been discussed in terms of familial relations. What, however, does this discussion suggest for concepts of citizenship?

Within biological constructions of the family, the understanding that identity is a social construction is often missing. Thus, the ways in which individual identity is embedded in community is also frequently absent. When identity is reduced to individuality, our ability to understand the interdependency of persons within a community, and of various communities with each other, is diminished. Again, in a participatory democracy, this has deleterious effects.

The value of identity, understood as individuality, teaches us to be distrustful of others unlike ourselves. Those who are unlike us seem to imply a critique of who we are and what we value. Thus we seek out others like ourselves. We avoid, and may even actively despise and persecute, those who deviate from what we hold to be true. Since we hold our own identity to be somehow "natural," those whose identity is different from ours must be unnatural.

The danger inherent in this value, as it is acted out within a pluralistic democracy, seems self-evident—we are reaping the fruits of such thinking in our current social climate. Racism has been part of our heritage from the earliest days of this country, and we find ourselves on the threshold of the twenty-first century still unable to rid ourselves of this scourge. Despite over two hundred years of "All men are created equal" we still cannot seem to create a collective commitment to this ideological goal.

Divisions along racial lines have historically been acted out in terms of white versus black, but other ethnicities have also been targeted. Asians have been accused of infiltrating our universities, taking more than their fair share of available slots. In California, Proposition 187 took aim at Hispanics (who, according to the rhetoric, use up our resources and deplete the available wealth), and Proposition 209 dismantled affirmative action.

When religious difference is added to racial/ethnic difference, we see an extension of intolerance. The bombing of the Federal Building in Oklahoma City provided telling evidence that this is the case. Scarcely had the dust settled when reports went out that this was the work of Muslim fundamentalist extremists. Talk-radio shows gave voice to hatred and scapegoating. Calls to "send them all back where they came from" could be heard. It is interesting to observe that when the real suspects turned out to be white reactionary militaristic extremists, nobody suggested deporting all white males.

Sexual diversity is yet another example of our intolerance. Lesbians and gay men are driven out of schools, the workplace, the military, and even our religious institutions. At one time it was even suggested that persons with AIDS, then identified as a homosexual disease, be rounded up and put in containment camps.

We are not offering here a simplistic answer to the problems of intolerance. The causes of racism, sexism, homophobia, anti-Semitism, etc., are deep and complex. However, we believe that a significant contributing factor is the lessons we learn early in our family of origin: to distrust those who are not our own, and to reserve our loyalties for those to whom we "belong."

Our failure to see our identity as a social construction cripples our ability to see our relation to others as an integral part of our own self-creation. As our social fabric has become increasingly diverse, the tensions caused by difference have been exacerbated and find expression in ever more violent and destructive actions. We seem, as a society, to become less tolerant, not more so.

The gay and lesbian communities are not immune to intolerance; the experience of being targeted because one is different does not necessarily lead to accepting the difference of others. But we do believe that this experience offers our communities a prophetic opportunity to practice the acceptance we demand for ourselves. Sadly, this opportunity is not often realized.

Difference does not threaten our common life together, but rather enhances it. In expanding the possibility for self-expression, difference provides more options for the discovery of identity. If we cannot teach this to our children, how will they secure a future society in a world where difference is unescapable? We will leave them the legacy of a fragmented society where competing interests vie for available resources, and where all persons and communities come up short.

Revaluing Erotic Power

We wish to comment briefly on the potential we believe erotic power has for the creation of a just society. Our religious and philosophical heritage has taught us to fear the erotic because it is identified as sexual and sensual. We have learned to distrust all passions which run deeply in our veins. Sexual behavior that does not conform to a narrowly defined standard of acceptability (heterosexual monogamy) is condemned.

Sensuality is distrusted because it is symbolic of weakness. We are told not to be deceived by our emotions. Our old puritan ethic remains to instill a suspicion of pleasure. At the same time the use of sexuality in advertisements and the media serves to reinforce the capitalist credo "Make a profit." Of course, that which is forbidden titillates, and titillation intrigues and sells.

In the midst of all this we have forgotten (if we ever knew) that the erotic is far more than sexuality, though it is also this. A revaluing of the erotic offers us at least two important lessons in citizenship. The first is to embrace passion. It is precisely those things which stir us most deeply that give us energy to sustain us in our work and to find joy in life. Without passion—passion for music, for art, for God, for laughter, for work, for love—life becomes grim drudgery. Why should anyone care to devote him- or herself to the work of justice if there is no passion in life?

The second lesson we can draw from erotic power is a reminder that we are all embodied beings. The value of erotic power calls us to revalue the physical nature of our lives, and the lives of all others in society. Women cannot be afraid of rape. Children cannot fear abuse. Gay men and lesbians cannot fear homophobic attacks. Whether we fear because of the color of our skin, or our sex, or our religious identity, or our economic security, these are all aspects of our physical existence. If we want a society in which people do not live in fear, we must teach future citizens that physical bodies, real human people, are sacred and that avoidable human suffering of any sort is sin.

Equally important to remember is that passion, sexuality, and sensuality are all physical experiences as well. Our physical well-being is every bit as important as our spiritual and psychological health; in fact, they cannot be divorced. In practical terms this means we must be committed to securing the well-being of all persons. Poverty and its attendant problems—hunger, disease, abuse—all hinder our ability to celebrate our physical existence. If there is no joy in life, there is no reason to commit to a future. There cannot be joy where there is fear for physical safety.

9

Conclusion: The Prophetic Nature of Gay and Lesbian Families

> God made from one blood all the families of earth,
> the circles of nurture that raised us from birth,
> companions who join us to work through each stage
> of childhood and youth and adulthood and age.
>
> We learn through families how our closeness and trust
> increase when our actions are loving and just
> yet families have also distorted their roles,
> mistreating their members and bruising their souls.
>
> Give, Lord, each family lost in conflict and storm
> a sense of your wisdom and grace that transform
> sharp anger to insight which strengthens the heart
> and makes clear the place where rebuilding can start.
>
> Make wide that wisdom and that grace to include
> the races and viewpoints our families exclude
> till peace in each home bears and nurtures the bud
> of peace shared by all you have made from one blood.
>
> —Thomas H. Troeger, "God Made from One Blood"[1]

Making Room for All?

To this point we have identified and critiqued the myth of the traditional family and the values that derive from it. We have provided a corrective to traditional family values, and suggested reasons why a transformation of family values is necessary for the good of society. In all of this, we have centered the experiences of lesbians and gay men and argued that family structures within our communities may provide a prophetic model for all of society. In this final chapter we wish to address two concerns. The first is to engage in critical self-reflection about our lesbian and gay communities, which often fall short of their prophetic promise. The second is to address the question of why we ought to embrace a pluralistic democracy as a good in its own right.

Diversity within the "Gay Family"

We are currently at an important point in gay and lesbian history. The political reaction against gay rights in the last decade is an indication of the strength of the gay community(ies). Lesbians and gay men are more visible and vocal than ever before. Openly gay men and lesbians are being elected to public office. We are doctors and lawyers and teachers and clergy and celebrities. Old stereotypes about homosexuals are publicly challenged and shattered. Lesbians and gay men are raising children, and raising them in homes where their parents refuse to be closeted. Straight parents have organized to support their lesbian and gay children (PFLAG). Thus, as we move into the twenty-first century, the potential we have claimed for our families has more possibility for actualization than ever before.

Throughout this work we have held up lesbian and gay family experiences as a framework within which to rethink family values. In so doing we have argued that these families may teach all of us less oppressive ways of relating within our families, lessons which may be transferred to our roles as citizens. However, we are also aware that the potential is not always realized. We are not naively idealistic in our claims, nor do we view our communities through the proverbial rose-colored glasses. We know that abuse exists within lesbian and gay families. We know that our communities are not free of racism, sexism, or classism. We know that often our families continue to perpetuate oppressive hierarchical structures. Thus we see this book as not only a critique of the dominant culture, but also a challenge to our own.

We do not, therefore, want to claim too much for these families. There are many forms of unjust hierarchies within our society, race, class, and gender being three of the most pervasive. Our claims about lesbian and gay families challenge gender issues directly. Traditional gender roles rest on the assumption that they are "natural"—that by nature men are one sort of creature and women are something entirely different. They also, as we have demonstrated, rely on the concept of gender complementarity, which suggests that men and women cannot be complete persons without the other.

The creation of lesbian and gay family structures calls into question traditional gender roles. In her book *Families We Choose,* Kath Weston noted that many of the people she interviewed "regarded equality as a distinguishing feature of relations within lesbian and gay couples."[2] Although some acknowledged various forms of role-playing within gay or lesbian relationships (for example, butch and femme roles among lesbians), these roles were not tied to the traditional gendered division of labor within the family. In fact, among lesbians who identified with butch and femme roles, these "identifications seldom coincided with divisions of labor in which only one partner worked outside the home."[3] According to Weston, lesbians and gay men overwhelmingly valued parity within their relationships, though not all agreed on what constituted an egalitarian relationship. These findings were borne out in our own interviews.

Because these traditional roles are hierarchical by definition, nonparticipation in these roles holds the potential for the creation of nonhierarchical models of mutuality in our intimate relationships. While these relationships also hold the potential for creating a critical sensibility about other forms of oppressive relationships premised on arguments from nature (for example, racist arguments), this potential, sadly, has yet to be realized.[4]

At a very basic level we are not surprised to find the failings of the broader society repeated in our midst, for this is the society we were raised in and where we learned our lessons of relationship. Simply coming to an awareness of lesbian/gay identity does not guarantee critical reflection on what it implies. In fact, society encourages us to divorce our personal lives from political analysis. Sexuality is described as a personal, individual matter, not a political issue. It is, we would argue, extremely difficult for most gay men and lesbians to see their identity as *completely* divorced from political implications, since both pro- and anti-gay measures continue to appear on election ballots. However, understanding that as a lesbian or a gay man you are denied certain basic rights in society is not the same thing as understanding that to be lesbian or gay is, at a deeper level, a political critique. Thus we often find that we continue to participate in the dominant cultural ideology while at the same time reacting against it.

Nevertheless, we would hold that the potential for lesbian and gay families to be transformative is significant. If we cannot unlearn hierarchy in our intimate relationships, relationships that at their best are characterized by love and commitment to others, how can we unlearn it and extend mutuality to broader social contexts where conflict is inescapable? If we cannot celebrate diversity among those we love, how will we tolerate it (much less embrace it) among those who are strangers?

The dismantling of gender roles within lesbian and gay families is a good place to start, offering society the opportunity to rethink family dynamics. But lesbian and gay communities must also turn a critical eye to the ways in which we continue to participate in other forms of hierarchy. Our communities are not immune to the pervasive racism that characterizes U.S. culture. We have noted that lesbians and gay men are increasingly claiming a public identity, "coming out of the closet" and demanding social recognition. We need to ask ourselves, however, why this is still a predominantly white, middle-class phenomenon. The ability to be public about one's sexual identity is accompanied by a degree of race privilege that often goes unaddressed. For the African American (or Latina/o or Asian) lesbian or gay man, existing in a culture where she or he is already stigmatized by race, coming out is a far more complex and dangerous proposition. Because homophobia cuts across ethnic and racial barriers, there is always the danger of alienation from one's own community. Since the dominant culture is racist, to be public about one's sexuality is to be doubly stigmatized. For the black lesbian in a sexist society, there is triple jeopardy.

Kath Weston's interviews revealed that fears springing from racism also continue to cause divisions within our communities. One gay black man pointed to this problem in his interaction with other gay men: "There's a possibility that if you walk up to them and talk to them, they're gonna say, 'I don't like black people.' So you have this perception of being attracted to this person who might *hate* you."[5]

We also find that issues of class continue to cause divisions within our communities, and again these issues operate from both without and within. On the one hand, outsiders often perceive lesbians and gay men as more economically privileged than most people, perhaps because those who receive the most public recognition are frequently celebrities or others who are extremely well-off (music mogul David Geffen is a good example). As Weston discovered, however, it also rests on the misconception that lesbians and gay men do not have families with children and therefore may selfishly spend their money on themselves.

Unfortunately, it seems to us, our own communities often perpetuate this image. By and large, magazines aimed at and published within our communities cater to the affluent among us. Advertisements for luxury cruises, elegant restaurants, and trendy nightclubs fill the pages. This critique needs to be made in the context of a consumer society where all persons are constantly bombarded with advertising designed to make us spend money we do not have on things we do not need. Nevertheless, we need to be more attuned to the economic realities of being gay and lesbian in the United States. Rampant homophobia does have a direct impact on the earning power of many within our communities. This is particularly true for lesbians, because women have historically enjoyed less economic mobility than men.

Another way that our communities participate in classist ideology is in the romanticization and eroticization of working-class folk. Within the gay community the blue-collar worker is sexualized as "virile"; within the lesbian community the butch woman is predominantly a working-class image. Both stereotypes lack sensitivity to the economic realities of working-class people. More than this, there is always the danger of objectifying working-class persons.

We also feel it is important to note the ways in which our communities participate in ageism and in what has been called "looksism." It is no secret, particularly within the gay community but also within lesbian circles, that youth and beauty are held at a premium. Although we may pay lip service to our elders, honoring them as pioneers in gay liberation, the reality is that "old dykes and fags" often find themselves alone. This is just another way in which we continue to participate in the dominant discourse which we claim to eschew.

We cannot complain about the homophobia in other communities unless we are willing to address the racism, sexism, classism, anti-Semitism, ageism, and other forms of discrimination within our own. We cannot take our "place at the table" if we are not willing to make room for others as well.

The Good of a Pluralistic Democracy

In addressing this final concern it is necessary to remind our readers of our own commitments and convictions. For both of us, Christian symbols and ideals continue to have power even as we recognize and struggle with the frequent abuses of that power. Thus, in this final section we allow ourselves to invoke the language of sin and redemption, justice and mercy, recognizing as we do that not all our readers will find similar meaning in this. We invite you to find your own metaphors.

We have argued that a transformation of values is necessary to equip future citizens to flourish in a pluralistic democracy. At one level this can be justified by purely utilitarian arguments, and there is certainly a long history of this kind of thinking within the tradition of social ethics in this country. Coming out of the Enlightenment, we find utilitarian arguments holding sway in public discourse about the good society. Stated simply, this is the principle that what makes a moral act right is that it produces the greatest good (or happiness) for the greatest number of people. In this sense, what is good is that course of action which is instrumental in producing the most happiness for the most people. It is not difficult for us to advance this kind of argument on behalf of pluralism. The reality is that we live in a society that is increasingly characterized by difference, and either we learn to negotiate these difficult waters or we will drown in them.

As critics of this approach have noted, however, the danger is that we create a morality in which, ultimately, the ends come to justify the means. In this case, we believe, there is also the danger that we fall prey to the fallacy of claiming that "what is" is what "ought to be." In other words, because we are "stuck" with pluralism, we better make the best of it. This denies the creative potential of humanity to envision ways of being that we may not yet experience. There are those who might claim that pluralism causes too many problems and the solution is to resist it as much as possible; to insist on conformity to a monolithic identity in order to avoid possible conflict. From this perspective, a strictly utilitarian argument could be made that all persons must fit into the model of the dominant group so as to cause the greatest comfort for the most people. Obviously, this would sacrifice the identity and experiences of many persons, including ourselves. Therefore, we believe that pluralism as a good must be defended on noninstrumental grounds.

We begin with the biblical creation myth, in which we are told that "God created man in his own image." For the point of our discussion, we choose to reread this statement in light of critiques made about male god-language, adopting a more inclusive perspective.[6] Thus, we might read this statement as "God created human beings in God's own image," and we understand this as a metaphor for the sanctity of all persons. If there is an element of the sacred in all human beings, then each and every person is a reflection of the divine, and it is in the totality of human existence that we discover God.

Our first premise, then, is that all persons are of value and worth and that no one person or group of persons has any greater claim to sacrality than any other. No one race, or gender, or religion, or sexuality is more godlike than another. No one has a divine right to rule. This understanding is in keeping with our commitment to mutuality as an appropriate model for human relationship. It undercuts hierarchical models of social organization, when such models are static and grant power and authority to one person or group of persons in perpetuity.

We believe that grounding our ethics in a foundation of human sacrality makes avoidable human suffering illegitimate as part of our body politic. Human suffering that is brought about by unjust power relations cannot be tolerated if we take seriously the symbolic significance that all persons are the image of God. To allow the suffering of others, when such suffering is unnecessary, is an offense not only against humanity but against God. To participate in the perpetuation of suffering is therefore sin.

A recognition of the sacrality of all persons not only requires a rejection of oppressive social structures. It also calls us to a celebration of difference within the human species. For if humanity is the image of God, then the divine creative impulse is neither singular nor static; it is a movement toward multiplicity and change. The variations within human experience which may surprise and delight us, and may trouble and confuse us, can be read as a reflection of the infinite possibilities of sacred expression.

To embrace pluralism, then, is to allow God to continually reveal Godself in new ways. Further, we would argue that increasing pluralism may be seen as the fulfilling of God's promise within human history. If God is a god of infinite possibility, then the greater the diversity among us, the greater the opportunity of discovering God in our midst. Christian faith is held together by its insistence on the significance of the incarnation, God made flesh among us. If we take this seriously, we must get away from the notion that this means only white flesh, or black flesh, or brown flesh, or straight flesh, or gay flesh. Flesh comes in multiple varieties. Thus, the symbolic meaning of the incarnation is that it takes all this flesh together to reveal the complete nature of God.

This notion, that the fullness of God is made manifest in a pluralistic society, serves as the foundation for our commitment to a participatory society. As we participate together in the communal enterprise called citizenship we discover the infinite nature of God expressed in the infinite possibilities of human nature. It is in reasoning together that we come to awareness of God's justice and mercy. Pluralism is not easy, and it requires humility. It calls us to a recognition that God can never be fully known; the divine nature can never fit into a neat little box. The sacred, as it is discovered in a diverse community, will often take us by surprise. This may frustrate us, it may anger us, but it can also delight.

If we continue to insist that there are only limited ways that God is revealed, only a finite number of possibilities for the manifestation of the sacred, we will continue to react against diversity. In so doing we, in essence, tell God who and what we will allow God to be. We set ourselves up as God, making God in our own image. The Bible calls this idolatry. The biblical prophet Micah tells us that God requires three things of us: that we do justice, that we love kindness, and that we walk humbly with our God (Micah 6:8). To do justice and love kindness in a pluralistic society demands that we put our collective and individual egos aside. It is the more difficult path to follow. But it is the journey we must begin.

Notes

1. Introduction: The Limits of Our Language

1. Throughout this book we will discuss both the "conservative right" and the "religious right," also sometimes referred to as political and religious conservatives, respectively. Although members of the religious right are also political conservatives, not all members of the conservative right ground their ideas in a religious worldview. The term "new right" is also used to describe the conflation of religious and political conservatives into a religio-political movement of the later twentieth century. Pamela Abbott and Claire Wallace maintain that the new right stresses "individual responsibility and the primacy of Christian moral values," and that it holds a "set of assumptions about the family and about the relationships between men and women." Pamela Abbott and Claire Wallace, *The Family and the New Right* (London: Pluto Press, 1992), 1. It is these assumptions, in particular, that we identify as the foundation of "traditional family values."
2. James Davison Hunter, *Culture Wars: The Struggle to Define America* (New York: Basic Books, 1991), 176.
3. Ibid., 177.
4. R. E. Allen, ed., *The Pocket Oxford Dictionary of Current English*, 7th ed. (Oxford: Clarendon Press, 1984), 265.
5. Nelle Morton, *The Journey Is Home* (Boston: Beacon Press, 1985), 20.
6. Betty Friedan, *The Feminine Mystique* (New York: W. W. Norton, 1963).
7. Susan Faludi, *Backlash: The Undeclared War against American Women* (New York: Crown Publishers, 1991), 53.
8. See, for example, the discussion of ideology in Catherine Belsey, *Critical Practice* (London: Methuen, 1980), 3 ff.
9. Quoted in Pamela Abbott and Claire Wallace, *The Family and the New Right*, 10.
10. Francis Goldsheider and Linda Waite, *New Families, No Family: The Transformation of the American Home* (Berkeley: University of California Press, 1991).
11. Susan Moller Okin, *Justice, Gender, and the Family* (New York: Basic Books, 1989).
12. David Popenoe, "American Family Decline, 1960–1990: A Review and Appraisal," *Journal of Marriage and the Family* 55 (1993): 527–55.
13. See, for example, Susan Moller Okin, *Justice, Gender, and the Family*, or Barrie Thorne and Marilyn Yalom, eds., *Rethinking the Family: Some Feminist Questions* (Boston: Northeastern University Press, 1992).

14. Carol B. Stack, *All Our Kin: Strategies for Survival in a Black Community* (New York: Harper & Row, 1970).
15. Barrie Thorne and Marilyn Yalom, eds., *Rethinking the Family: Some Feminist Questions.*
16. Kath Weston, *Families We Choose* (New York: Columbia University Press, 1991).
17. Gerda Lerner, *The Creation of Patriarchy* (New York: Oxford University Press, 1986), 121.
18. Jean Bethke Elshtain, "Introduction: Toward a Theory of the Family and Politics," in Elshtain, *The Family in Political Thought* (Amherst: University of Massachusetts Press, 1982), 7–30, 12.
19. Aristotle, *The Politics*, trans. Carnes Lord (Chicago: University of Chicago Press, 1984), book 1, ch. 2, p. 37.
20. Ibid., book 1, ch. 13, p. 54.
21. Wayne A. Meeks, *The First Urban Christians: The Social World of the Apostle Paul* (New Haven, Conn.: Yale University Press, 1983), 30.
22. St. Augustine, the Bishop of Hippo, 354–430 C.E. The work of Augustine is important to an understanding of Christian theology because of his historical location. He was influential in the shaping of Roman Catholic thought at a crucial point in its history, at the time when the Christian faith became the official religion of the Roman Empire. Perhaps more than any other single thinker of his time, his ideas about the relationship of church and state would become definitive for western Europe throughout the Middle Ages.
23. Augustine, *City of God*, ed. David Knowles, trans. Henry Bettenson (New York: Penguin Books, 1972), book 19, chs. 14–15.
24. Ibid., ch. 16.
25. Augustine, *The Confessions*, trans. Edward B. Pusey (New York: Quality Paperback Book Club, 1991), 125.
26. Jean-Louis Flandrin, *Families in Former Times: Kinship, Household, and Sexuality*, trans. Richard Southern (Cambridge: Cambridge University Press, 1979); Philippe Ariès, *Centuries of Childhood: A Social History of Family Life*, trans. Robert Baldick (New York: Vintage Books, 1962).
27. Martin Luther, *Lectures on Genesis: Chapter 1–5*, in *Luther's Works*, vol. 1, ed. Jaroslav Pelikan (St. Louis: Concordia Publishing House, 1958), Gen. 2:18, p. 115.
28. Martin Luther, "The Estate of Marriage," in Elizabeth Clark and Herbert Richardson, eds., *Women and Religion: A Feminist Sourcebook of Christian Thought* (New York: Harper & Row, 1977), 135.
29. Martin Luther, "A Sermon on the Estate of Marriage," in *Martin Luther's Basic Theological Writings*, ed. Timothy F. Lull (Minneapolis: Fortress Press, 1989), 630–37, 635.

30. Martin Luther, *Lectures on Genesis: Chapters 1–5*, in *Luther's Works*, vol. 1, Gen. 2:22, p. 134.
31. Ariès, *Centuries of Childhood,* 404.
32. Carole Pateman, *The Sexual Contract* (Stanford, Calif.: Stanford University Press, 1988).
33. Okin, *Justice, Gender, and the Family,* 33.
34. We use America in its more localized sense here, referring to the United States of America.
35. Stephanie Coontz, *The Social Origins of Private Life: A History of American Families, 1600–1900* (New York: Verso Press, 1988).
36. Ibid., 354–55.
37. Carol A. B. Warren, *Madwives: Schizophrenic Women in the 1950s* (New Brunswick, N.J.: Rutgers University Press, 1987).
38. Ariès, *Centuries of Childhood,* 407.
39. Gayatri Chakravorty Spivak, *The Post-Colonial Critic*, ed. Sarah Harasym (New York: Routledge, 1990), 41.

2. Fidelity

1. The value of monogamy has generally applied more strictly to women than men as a means for men to control women's sexuality. See, for example, the special section "Feminism and Family Values" in the *Journal of Feminist Studies in Religion* 12, no. 1 (spring 1996); Okin, *Justice, Gender, and the Family;* Pateman, *The Sexual Contract.*
2. Jim Cotter, "The Gay Challenge to Traditional Notions of Human Sexuality," in *Towards a Theology of Gay Liberation,* ed. Malcolm Macourt (London: SCM Press, 1977), 71.
3. Sissela Bok, 1978, *Lying: Moral Choice in Public and Private Life* (New York: Vintage Books), 33.
4. Zygmunt Bauman, *Postmodern Ethics* (Oxford: Blackwell Publishers, 1993), 98.
5. Ibid.
6. Lillian B. Rubin, *Just Friends: The Role of Friendship in Our Lives* (New York: Harper & Row, 1986), 5.
7. Ibid., 13.
8. Linda A. Moody, *Women Encounter God: Theology across the Boundaries of Difference* (New York: Orbis Books, 1996), 149.
9. Robert N. Bellah et al., *The Good Society* (New York: Alfred A. Knopf, 1991), 261.

10. John Preston, ed., *Hometowns: Gay Men Write About Where They Belong* (New York: Dutton, 1991), xii.
11. Ethan Mordden, *Buddies* (New York: St. Martin's Press, 1986), 189.

3. Mutuality and Accountability

1. James B. Nelson, *Between Two Gardens: Reflections on Sexuality and Religious Experience* (New York: The Pilgrim Press, 1983), 130.
2. Rodney Clapp, *Families at the Crossroads: Beyond Traditional and Modern Options* (Downers Grove, Ill.: InterVarsity Press, 1993), 13. It is worth noting that even this evangelical author, writing for a decidedly conservative Christian press, finds fault with this idealization of the family.
3. Ibid., 86.
4. Weston, *Families We Choose,* 192.
5. Beverly Wildung Harrison, "Sexism and the Language of Christian Ethics," in Beverly Wildung Harrison, *Making the Connections: Essays in Feminist Social Ethics,* ed. Carol S. Robb (Boston: Beacon Press, 1985), 37.
6. Ibid., 39.
7. Sarah Lucia Hoagland, *Lesbian Ethics: Toward New Value* (Palo Alto, Calif.: Institute of Lesbian Studies, 1988), 75.
8. Ibid., 86.
9. Clapp, *Families at the Crossroads,* 86.
10. Interview with Stone Phillips on the television program *Dateline,* August 11, 1992, NBC.
11. The work of the Stone Center is discussed in Carter Heyward, *Touching Our Strength: The Erotic as Power and the Love of God* (San Francisco: HarperSanFrancisco, 1989), 13.
12. Ibid., 17.
13. Mary E. Hunt, *Fierce Tenderness: A Feminist Theology of Friendship* (New York: Crossroad, 1991), 29.
14. Okin, *Justice, Gender, and the Family.*
15. Ibid., 8.
16. Beverly Wildung Harrison, "Misogyny and Homophobia: The Unexplored Connections," in *Making the Connections,* 149–50.
17. Okin, *Justice, Gender, and the Family.*
18. See, for example, Michèle Barrett and Mary McIntosh, *The Anti-social Family* (London: NLB, 1982).
19. Hoagland, *Lesbian Ethics,* 29.
20. Carter Heyward, "Heterosexism: Enforcing Male Supremacy," in *Redefining Sexual Ethics: A Sourcebook of Essays, Stories, and Poems,* ed. Susan E. Davies and Eleanor H. Haney (Cleveland: The Pilgrim Press, 1991), 103–13.

21. Heyward, *Touching Our Strength*, 34.
22. Ibid., 35.
23. Kristine M. Baber and Katherine R. Allen, *Women and Families: Feminist Reconstructions* (New York/London: The Guilford Press, 1992).
24. Ibid., 24.
25. Heyward, *Touching Our Strength*, 106.

4. Giving Life

1. *Newsweek*, Nov. 4, 1996 (on-line).
2. Carole S. Collum, "Co-parent Adoptions: Lesbian and Gay Parenting," *Trial* 29, no. 6 (1993): 28–34.
3. Okin, *Justice, Gender, and the Family*, 160.
4. Weston, *Families We Choose*, 187–88.
5. "Homosexuality Does Not Make Parent Unfit, Court Rules," *New York Times*, June 22, 1994, A8.
6. In another recent case, the Supreme Court appears to have moved away from appeals to natural law and/or claims concerning the Judeo/Christian tradition in its legal reasoning. In *Michael H. v. Gerald D.* (1989) the court denied parental visitation rights to Michael H., the biological father of the child in question. When the child was born, the child's mother was married to another man. A state statute held that the man to whom the woman was married when the child was born was the legitimate father. As Richard Mohr comments, one might have thought the court would have based its reasoning on some notion of natural law and given rights to the biological father. Although conservative doctrine defines the family as a natural institution with roots in human biology, the court's ruling indicates that the family is a social construction bounded and defined by law. Richard D. Mohr, *Gay Ideas: Outing and Other Controversies* (Boston: Beacon Press, 1992), 67–68.
7. Isaiah Crawford and Elizabeth Solliday, "The Attitudes of Undergraduate College Students toward Gay Parenting" *Journal of Homosexuality* 30, no. 4 (1996): 63–77.
8. See, for example, Sherri B. Victor and Marian C. Fish, "Lesbian Mothers and Their Children: A Review for School Psychologists," *School Psychology Review* 24, no. 3 (1995): 456–79; Robert L. Barret and Bryan E. Robinson, *Gay Fathers* (Lexington, Mass.: Lexington Books, 1990), 149–54; Jerry J. Bigner and Brooke R. Jacobsen, "Parenting Behaviors of Homosexual and Heterosexual Fathers," *Journal of Homosexuality* 18, nos. 1–2 (1989): 174–86, and "Adult Responses to Child Behavior and Attitudes toward Fathering: Gay and Non-gay Fathers," *Journal of Homosexuality* 23, no. 3 (1992): 99–112.

9. *Newsweek*, Nov. 4, 1996 (on-line).
10. Laura Berkov, *Reinventing the Family: The Emerging Story of Lesbian and Gay Parents* (New York: Crown Publishers, 1994), 2–3.
11. Research conducted by Julie Ainslie and Kathryn Felty echoes Sandy and Barb's experience. "Definitions and Dynamics of Motherhood and Families in Lesbian Communities," *Marriage and Family Review* 17, no. 1–2 (1991): 63–85.
12. Phyllis Burke, *Family Values: A Lesbian Mother's Fight for Her Son* (New York: Vintage Books, 1993).
13. Dorothy E. Smith, "The Standard North American Family," *Journal of Family Issues* 14 (1993): 50–65.
14. Anna G. Jonasdottir, *Why Women Are Oppressed* (Philadelphia: Temple University Press, 1994), 156.
15. Elizabeth A. Say, *Evidence on Her Own Behalf: Women's Narrative as Theological Voice* (Savage, Md.: Rowan & Littlefield, 1990), 100.
16. Betty Friedan, *The Fountain of Age* (New York: Simon & Schuster, 1993), 620.
17. Andrew Sullivan, *Virtually Normal: An Argument about Homosexuality* (New York: Vintage Books, 1995), 201.

5. Identity and Community

1. Edmund White, *A Boy's Own Story* (New York: Quality Paperback Book Club, 1982), 27.
2. The PFLAG national office is located in Washington, D.C.; the phone number is (202) 638-4200.
3. Peter Berger and Thomas Luckman, *The Social Construction of Reality: A Treatise in the Sociology of Knowledge* (New York: Doubleday & Co., 1966), 173.
4. Bruce Bawer, "Sex-Negative Me," in *Beyond Queer: Challenging Gay Left Orthodoxy*, ed. Bruce Bawer (New York: The Free Press, 1996), 171–73, 173.
5. Norah Vincent, "Beyond Lesbian," in *Beyond Queer*, 181–85, 182.

6. Erotic Power

1. Eleanor H. Haney, "Sexual Being—Burden and Possibility: A Feminist Reflection on Sexual Ethics," in *Redefining Sexual Ethics*, 229–51.
2. Jerry Falwell, *Listen, America!* (New York: Bantam Books, 1981), 110–11, cited in Helen Hardacre, "The Impact of Fundamentalisms on Women, the Family, and Interpersonal Relations," in *Fundamentalisms and Society: Reclaiming the Sciences, the Family, and Education*, ed. Martin E. Marty and R. Scott Appleby (Chicago: University of Chicago Press, 1993).

3. Haney, "Sexual Being," 233.
4. Audre Lorde, "Uses of the Erotic: The Erotic as Power," in *Weaving the Visions: New Patterns in Feminist Spirituality*, ed. Judith Plaskow and Carol P. Christ (San Francisco: Harper & Row, 1989), 208–13, 210.
5. Rita Nakashima Brock, *Journeys by Heart: A Christology of Erotic Power* (New York: Crossroad, 1988), 40.
6. Ibid.
7. Ibid., 35.

7. Marriage and Family

1. Charles Eric Reeves, "Vice-Versa: Rhetorical Reflections in an Ideological Mirror," *New Literary History* 23 (1992): 159–71, 168.
2. Paula L. Ettelbrick, "Since When Is Marriage a Path to Liberation?," in *Lesbian and Gay Marriage: Private Commitments, Public Ceremonies,* ed. Suzanne Sherman (Philadelphia: Temple University Press, 1992), 21.
3. Thomas Stoddard, "Why Gay People Should Seek the Right to Marry," in *Lesbian and Gay Marriage,* 13–19.
4. Nan Hunter, quoted in William N. Eskridge, *The Case for Same-Sex Marriage* (New York: The Free Press, 1996), 61.
5. Eskridge, *The Case for Same-Sex Marriage,* 65.
6. "Same-Sex Marriage: Federal and States Authority," *Congressional Digest*, vol. 75, no. 11 (1996): 263, 288.
7. Ibid., 263.
8. Ibid.
9. Sullivan, *Virtually Normal,* 182–83.
10. Bruce Bawer, *A Place at the Table: The Gay Individual in American Society* (New York: Poseidon Press), 252 ff.

8. (Re)Politicizing the Family

1. *The Oxford Encyclopedic English Dictionary*, ed. Joyce M. Hawkins and Robert Allen (Oxford: Clarendon Press, 1991), 384.

9. Conclusion: The Prophetic Nature of Gay and Lesbian Families

1. Thomas H. Troeger, "God Made from One Blood," from *New Hymns for the Life of the Church* (New York: Oxford University Press, 1988). According to Robert G. Stapp, director of music at Lakeshore Avenue Baptist Church in

Oakland, California, "This text was commissioned . . . to provide a hymn that recognizes the many different kinds of families that are represented when a campus congregation gathers to worship."

2. Weston, *Families We Choose,* 149.
3. Ibid.
4. One of the most disturbing recent examples of this form of argument is Richard J. Herrnstein and Charles Murray, *The Bell Curve: Intelligence and Class Structure in American Life* (New York: The Free Press, 1994).
5. Weston, *Families We Choose,* 144.
6. Such critiques recognize that language is a tool of power and reflects the experiences and values of those who hold power; historically, this has been privileged males. We are aware that simply broadening the category of "man" to "humankind" does not divorce this from the power dynamics. Recent scholarship, however, does seem to indicate that this more inclusive reading is actually more in keeping with the original Hebrew text. See, for example, Phyllis Trible, *God and the Rhetoric of Sexuality* (Philadelphia: Fortress Press, 1978).

Bibliography

Abbott, Pamela, and Claire Wallace. *The Family and the New Right.* London: Pluto Press, 1992.

Ainslie, Julie, and Kathryn Felty. "Definitions and Dynamics of Motherhood and Families in Lesbian Communities." *Marriage and Family Review* 17, nos. 1–2 (1991): 63–85.

Ariès, Philippe. *Centuries of Childhood: A Social History of Family Life.* Translated by Robert Baldick. New York: Vintage Books, 1962.

Aristotle. *The Politics.* Translated by Carnes Lord. Chicago: University of Chicago Press, 1984.

Augustine. *City of God.* Edited by David Knowles. Translated by Henry Bettenson. New York: Penguin Books, 1972.

———. *The Confessions.* Translated by Edward B. Pusey. New York: Quality Paperback Book Club, 1991.

Baber, Kristine M., and Katherine R. Allen. *Women and Families: Feminist Reconstructions.* New York/London: The Guilford Press: 1992.

Barret, Robert L., and Bryan E. Robinson. *Gay Fathers.* Lexington, Mass.: Lexington Books, 1990.

Barrett, Michèle, and Mary McIntosh. *The Anti-social Family.* London: NLB, 1982.

Bauman, Zygmunt. *Postmodern Ethics.* Oxford: Blackwell Publishers, 1993.

Bawer, Bruce. "Sex-Negative Me." In *Beyond Queer: Challenging Gay Left Orthodoxy,* edited by Bruce Bawer. New York: The Free Press, 1996.

———. *A Place at the Table: The Gay Individual in American Society.* New York: Poseidon Press, 1993.

Bellah, Robert N., et al. *The Good Society.* New York: Alfred A. Knopf, 1991.

Belsey, Catherine. *Critical Practice.* London: Methuen, 1980.

Benkov, Laura. *Reinventing the Family: The Emerging Story of Lesbian and Gay Parents.* New York: Crown Publishers, 1994.

Berger, Peter, and Thomas Luckman. *The Social Construction of Reality: A Treatise in the Sociology of Knowledge.* New York: Doubleday, 1966.

Bigner, Jerry J., and Brooke R. Jacobsen. "Parenting Behaviors of Homosexual and Heterosexual Fathers." *Journal of Homosexuality* 18, nos. 1–2 (1989): 174–86.

———. "Adult Responses to Child Behavior and Attitudes toward Fathering: Gay and Non-gay Fathers." *Journal of Homosexuality* 23, no. 3 (1992): 99–112.

Bok, Sissela. *Lying: Moral Choice in Public and Private Life.* New York: Vintage Books, 1978.

Brock, Rita Nakashima. *Journeys by Heart: A Christology of Erotic Power.* New York: Crossroad, 1988.

Burke, Phyllis. *Family Values: A Lesbian Mother's Fight for Her Son.* New York: Vintage Books, 1993.

Clapp, Rodney. *Families at the Crossroads: Beyond Traditional and Modern Options.* Downers Grove, Ill.: InterVarsity Press, 1993.

Clark, Elizabeth, and Herbert Richardson, eds. *Women and Religion: A Feminist Sourcebook of Christian Thought.* New York: Harper & Row, 1977.

Collum, Carole S. "Co-parent Adoptions: Lesbian and Gay Parenting." *Trial* 29, no. 6 (1993): 28–34.

Coontz, Stephanie. *The Social Origins of Private Life: A History of American Families, 1600–1900.* New York: Verso Press, 1988.

Cotter, Jim. "The Gay Challenge to Traditional Notions of Human Sexuality." In *Towards a Theology of Gay Liberation,* edited by Malcolm Macourt. London: SCM Press, 1977.

Crawford, Isaiah, and Elizabeth Solliday. "The Attitudes of Undergraduate College Students toward Gay Parenting." *Journal of Homosexuality* 30, no. 4 (1996): 63–77.

Elshtain, Jean Bethke. *The Family in Political Thought.* Amherst: University of Massachusetts Press, 1982.

Eskridge, William N. *The Case for Same-Sex Marriage.* New York: The Free Press, 1996.

Ettelbrick, Paula L. "Since When Is Marriage a Path to Liberation?" In *Lesbian and Gay Marriage: Private Commitments, Public Ceremonies,* edited by Suzanne Sherman. Philadelphia: Temple University Press, 1992.

Faludi, Susan. *Backlash: The Undeclared War against American Women.* New York: Crown Publishers, 1991.

Flandrin, Jean-Louis. *Families in Former Times: Kinship, Household, and Sexuality.* Translated by Richard Southern. Cambridge: Cambridge University Press, 1979.

Friedan, Betty. *The Feminine Mystique.* New York: W. W. Norton, 1963.

———. *The Fountain of Age.* New York: Simon & Schuster, 1993.

Golvin, Sandra. "Chinese Medicine." In *Hers: Brilliant New Fiction by Lesbian Writers,* edited by Terry Wolverton and Robert Drake. Winchester, Mass.: Faber & Faber, 1995.

Goldsheider, Frances, and Linda Waite. *New Families, No Family: The Transformation of the American Home.* Berkeley: University of California Press, 1991.

Haney, Eleanor H. "Sexual Being—Burden and Possibility: A Feminist Reflection on Sexual Ethics." In *Redefining Sexual Ethics: A Sourcebook of Essays, Stories, and Poems,* edited by Susan E. Davies and Eleanor H. Haney. Cleveland: The Pilgrim Press, 1991.

Hardacre, Helen. "The Impact of Fundamentalisms on Women, the Family, and Interpersonal Relations." In *Fundamentalisms and Society: Reclaiming the Sciences, the Family, and Education*, edited by Martin E. Marty and R. Scott Appleby. Chicago: University of Chicago Press, 1993.

Harrison, Beverly Wildung. *Making the Connections: Essays in Feminist Social Ethics.* Edited by Carol S. Robb. Boston: Beacon Press, 1985.

Herrnstein, Richard J., and Charles Murray. *The Bell Curve: Intelligence and Class Structure in American Life.* New York: The Free Press, 1994.

Heyward, Carter. *Touching Our Strength: The Erotic as Power and the Love of God.* San Francisco: HarperSanFrancisco, 1989.

———. "Heterosexism: Enforcing Male Supremacy." In *Redefining Sexual Ethics: A Sourcebook of Essays, Stories, and Poems*, edited by Susan E. Davies and Eleanor H. Haney. Cleveland: The Pilgrim Press, 1991.

Hoagland, Sarah Lucia. *Lesbian Ethics: Toward New Value.* Palo Alto, Calif.: Institute of Lesbian Studies, 1988.

Hunt, Mary E. *Fierce Tenderness: A Feminist Theology of Friendship.* New York: Crossroad, 1991.

Hunter, James Davison. *Culture Wars: The Struggle to Define America.* New York: Basic Books, 1991.

Jonasdottir, Anna G. *Why Women Are Oppressed.* Philadelphia: Temple University Press, 1994.

Lerner, Gerda. *The Creation of Patriarchy.* New York: Oxford University Press, 1991.

Luther, Martin. *Lectures on Genesis: Chapters 1–5.* In *Luther's Works*, vol. 1, edited by Jaroslav Pelikan. St. Louis: Concordia Publishing House, 1958.

———. "A Sermon on the Estate of Marriage." In *Martin Luther's Basic Theological Writings*, edited by Timothy F. Lull. Minneapolis: Fortress Press, 1989.

Lorde, Audre. "Uses of the Erotic: The Erotic as Power." In *Weaving the Visions: New Patterns in Feminist Spirituality*, edited by Judith Plaskow and Carol P. Christ. San Francisco: Harper & Row, 1989.

Meeks, Wayne A. *The First Urban Christians: The Social World of the Apostle Paul.* New Haven, Conn.: Yale University Press, 1983.

Moody, Linda A. *Women Encounter God: Theology across the Boundaries of Difference.* New York: Orbis Books, 1996.

Mohr, Richard D. *Gay Ideas: Outing and Other Controversies.* Boston: Beacon Press, 1992.

Mordden, Ethan. *Buddies.* New York: St. Martin's Press, 1986.

Morton, Nelle. *The Journey Is Home.* Boston: Beacon Press, 1985.

Newlson, James B. *Between Two Gardens: Reflections on Sexuality and Religious Experience.* New York: The Pilgrim Press, 1983.

Okin, Susan Moller. *Justice, Gender, and the Family.* New York: Basic Books, 1989.

Pateman, Carole. *The Sexual Contract.* Stanford, Calif.: Stanford University Press, 1988.

Popenoe, David. "American Family Decline, 1960–1990: A Review and Appraisal." *Journal of Marriage and the Family* 55 (1993): 527–55.

Preston, John, ed. *Hometowns: Gay Men Write About Where They Belong.* New York: Dutton, 1991.

Reeves, Charles Eric. "Vice-Versa: Rhetorical Reflections in an Ideological Mirror." *New Literary History* 23 (1992): 159–71.

Rubin, Lillian B. *Just Friends: The Role of Friendship in Our Lives.* New York: Harper & Row, 1986.

"Same-Sex Marriage: Federal and States Authority." *Congressional Digest* 75, no. 11 (1996): 263–88.

Say, Elizabeth A. *Evidence on Her Own Behalf: Women's Narrative as Theological Voice.* Savage, Md.: Roman & Littlefield, 1990.

Smith, Dorothy E. "The Standard North American Family." *Journal of Family Issues* 14 (1993): 50–65.

Spivak, Gayatri Chakravorty. *The Post-Colonial Critic.* Edited by Sarah Harasym. New York: Routledge, 1990.

Stack, Carol B. *All Our Kin: Strategies for Survival in a Black Community.* New York: Harper & Row, 1970.

Stoddard, Thomas. "Why Gay People Should Seek the Right to Marry." In *Lesbian and Gay Marriage: Private Commitments, Public Ceremonies,* edited by Suzanne Sherman. Philadelphia: Temple University Press, 1992.

Sullivan, Andrew. *Virtually Normal: An Argument about Homosexuality.* New York: Vintage Books, 1995.

Thorne, Barrie, and Marilyn Yalom, eds. *Rethinking the Family: Some Feminist Questions.* Boston: Northeastern University Press, 1992.

Trible, Phyllis. *God and the Rhetoric of Sexuality.* Philadelphia: Fortress Press, 1978.

Troeger, Thomas H. "God Made from One Blood." Oxford University Press Inc., 1988. In *A New Hymnal for Colleges and Schools,* edited by Jeffery Rowthorn and Russell Schultz-Widmar. New Haven and London: Yale University Press, in association with the Yale Institute of Sacred Music, 1992.

Victor, Sherri B., and Marian C. Fish. "Lesbian Mothers and Their Children: A Review for School Psychologists." *School Psychology Review* 24, no. 3 (1995): 456–79.

Vincent, Norah. "Beyond Lesbian." In *Beyond Queer: Challenging Gay Left Orthodoxy,* edited by Bruce Bawer. New York: The Free Press, 1996.

Warren, Carol A. B. *Madwives: Schizophrenic Women in the 1950s.* New Brunswick, N.J.: Rutgers University Press, 1987.

Weston, Kath. *Families We Choose.* New York: Columbia University Press, 1991.

White, Edmund. *A Boy's Own Story.* New York: Quality Paperback Book Club, 1982.

Index